Looking
in All the Right
Directions

Pastor Chuck's Final Messages
to His Congregation

Five Sermons on 2 Timothy
Delivered September to October 2024

Charles R. Swindoll

INSIGHT FOR LIVING

The Bible-Teaching Ministry of Pastor Charles R. Swindoll

LOOKING IN ALL THE RIGHT DIRECTIONS
Pastor Chuck's Final Messages to His Congregation
by Charles R. Swindoll

ACKNOWLEDGMENTS

Book content was adapted by Insight for Living staff from the original outlines and transcripts from the sermon series, *Looking in All the Right Directions*, Copyright © 2024 by Charles R. Swindoll, Inc.

President, Insight for Living: Charissa Swindoll Gaither

Senior Vice President, Communications and Engagement: Linda Ricks, BBA, Marketing and Accounting, Baylor University

Senior Vice President, *Searching the Scriptures* Ministries: Aaron Massey, ThM, Dallas Theological Seminary

Vice President, *Searching the Scriptures* Ministries: Bryce Klabunde, ThM, Dallas Theological Seminary; DMin, Western Seminary

Substantive Editor: Jim Craft, MA, English, Mississippi College; MA, Christian Studies, Dallas Theological Seminary

Print Communications Manager, Publishing: Autumn Swindoll, BA, Humanities, Biola University

Production Editor: Katie Hayes, BA, Communications, Southwest Baptist University

Proofreader: Joni Halpin, BS, Accounting, Miami University

Graphic Designer: Laura Dubroc, BFA, Advertising Design, University of Louisiana at Lafayette

Production Artist: Nancy Gustine, BFA, Advertising Art, University of North Texas

ISBN: 978-1-62655-242-5

Printed in the United States of America

CONTENTS

INTRODUCTION

In the dimming light of a life lived for others, few individuals shine as brightly as my father, Chuck Swindoll. With an incredible journey spanning sixty years of ministry, he stepped away from the pulpit at the remarkable age of 90, leaving behind an indelible legacy at Stonebriar Community Church in Frisco, Texas—a place he founded and nurtured with steadfast love and purpose. The heart of his last five messages resonates throughout these pages, a compilation not merely of sermons but a heartfelt discourse of wisdom and vulnerability from a man who has not only taught us about God but has also lived an exemplary life.

Chuck reminisces in these messages, casting his gaze back over valleys climbed and mountains weathered. He reflects on the mentors who shaped him—figures who offered guidance, encouragement, and accountability along his spiritual journey. As Paul penned the epistle to Timothy from a dark cell, facing the end of his life, Chuck, too, draws from his own experiences, encapsulating in poignant fashion the fibers of grace and faith that have stitched together the fabric of his life.

Being a pastor is no soft calling; it's a battleground where the soldier of Christ withstands arrows of doubt and disdain. The lives touched, messages delivered, and hard truths shared are not for the fainthearted. Chuck knows this all too well. I'll never forget the stories he's relayed about the pivotal moments in his life—like the time he found himself in a Marine Corps barrack—feeling utterly lost, until a wise mentor spoke into his life, "You are a leader!" Those words breathed life into a vision that would carve out a path for generations to follow. It was that early empowering influence, that unyielding faith in him, that drove Chuck to answer God's calling head-on, paving a way to becoming a pastor who has inspired millions around the world.

Chuck candidly acknowledges the reality that while Christianity calls for grace and unity, it also thrusts us into a crucible that refines human imperfection. His experiences reveal that there may be moments where we feel warfare being waged not only by external forces but also from within our own congregations. Yet through it all, he strives to remain authentic and humble with unwavering resolve. To lead effectively, one must wear his or her scars openly and acknowledge weaknesses, for a great leader reveals not only his or her strengths but also admits his or her vulnerabilities.

In these challenging times, when so many churches and ministries drift in the winds of culture, Chuck offers fresh insights into the timeless principles leaders need to rely on to guide the people entrusted to them. His conviction is simple yet profound: as pastors and believers, we must stand firm against the tides of cultural change, not cower in fear but move forward in faith. We must focus on what truly matters: living lives marked by fidelity to Christ's message in a world that often contradicts and despises it.

As I reflect on this compelling conclusion to my father's ministry, I cannot help but be awed by his integrity, a rare commodity in a world increasingly devoid of such virtue. For all his faults—which he freely admits—he has been a solid anchor of authenticity in a stormy sea. I have never doubted his integrity nor questioned his sincerity or commitment to our family. I have never known my father to lie, nor has he broken the hearts of those closest to him when he could have easily served himself.

In these pages, you will find not only the legacy of a faithful servant but also a resounding call to each of us: to endure, to remember, and to lead with hearts that are both tender and steadfast. As Chuck Swindoll closes this monumental chapter, he invites you to lean in, listen closely, and take to heart the lessons he's learned along the way. For as we chart and follow our own trajectories, each of us carries the torch of guidance handed to us by others. Let us walk with integrity, resilience, and an unwavering focus on eternity.

> Joining you in taking on life with a great attitude!
>
> Charissa Swindoll Gaither
> President
> Insight for Living

Looking
in All the Right
Directions

Pastor Chuck's Final Messages
to His Congregation

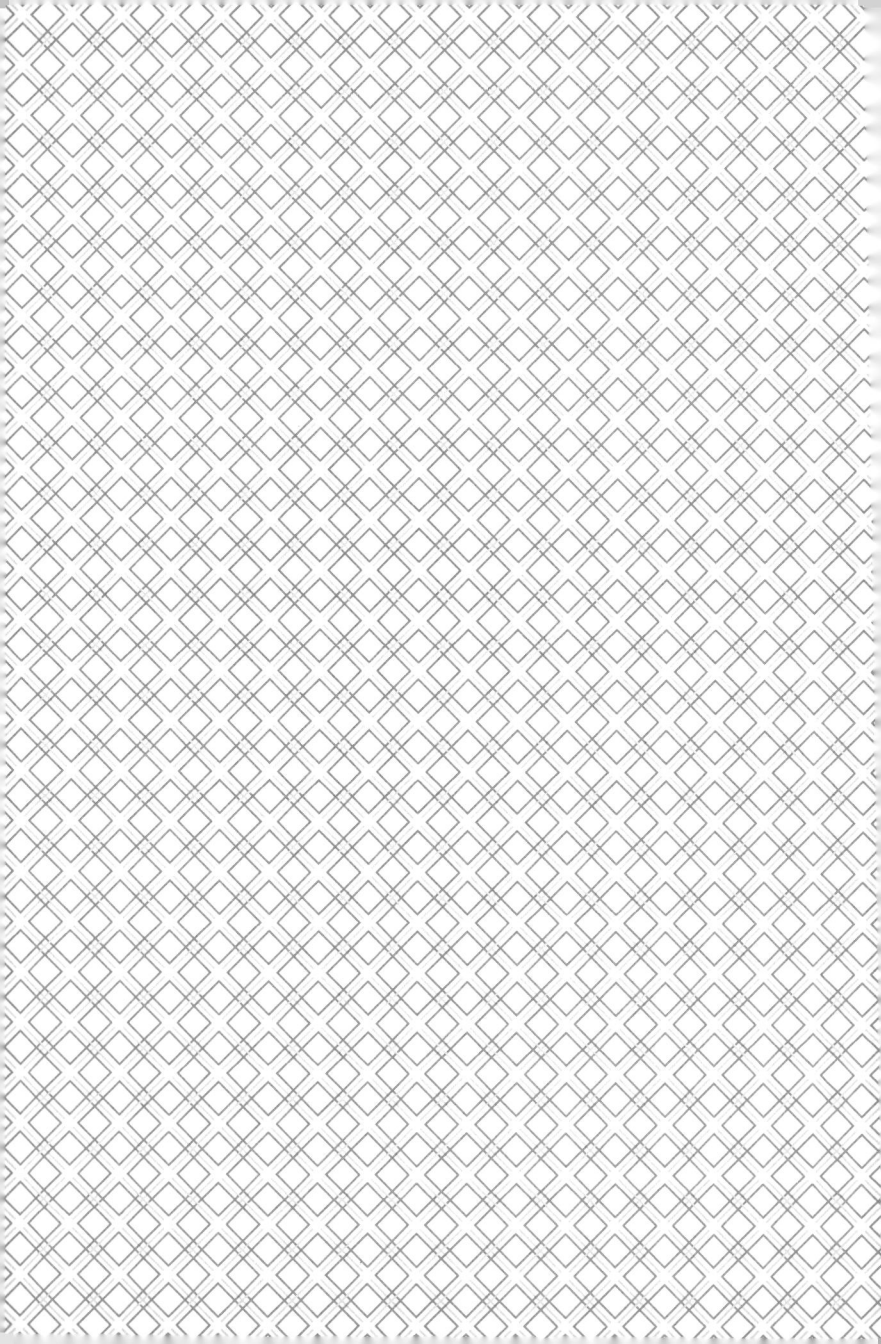

CHAPTER 1

Look Back
Who Were Your Mentors?

Delivered September 22, 2024

*I remember your genuine faith, for you share
the faith that first filled your grandmother Lois and
your mother, Eunice. And I know that same
faith continues strong in you.*
2 TIMOTHY 1:5

Who would have expected Paul to finish his ministry in a dungeon? Not just any dungeon, but the worst prison in Rome, shoulder-to-shoulder with the most violent criminals. How did he end up here?

At the time, the Roman Empire was ruled by the madman, Nero. After a massive fire destroyed half of Rome, rumors spread that he set the fire to clear space for his own building projects. Nero deflected blame by accusing Christians of causing the fire and inciting a mass persecution of them. Anyone who worshiped Jesus as Lord was considered an enemy of the empire. In terrorizing raids, the emperor's troops rounded up as many Christians as they could find. Nero ordered some to be devoured by wild animals before a bloodthirsty crowd, and others he had doused in oil and set ablaze to light his gardens.

The dragnet of Nero's persecution eventually caught Paul who was arrested as a Christian ringleader. Nero threw Paul into the notorious Mamertine Prison to await a rigged trial and certain execution.

The dungeon was once a subterranean cistern—a foul-smelling, cold, dark cavern. The only light in the dungeon came through a grate above Paul, like an oversized manhole. It was like living in an open sewer. The stench of human excrement filled the pungent air, stinging the nostrils. I don't know how Paul stood it.

Paul's Last Words

Paul was about 65 years old—his hair white, his face wrinkled, his back bent, his body scarred. We don't know how long he languished in prison, but we do know that he wrote the Second Letter to Timothy from that horrid place.

If final words are important words, then these four chapters contain among the most important words from Paul. They are his swan song, his last and most personal words before his death.

Paul wrote with deep emotion. "Only Luke is with me," Paul scratched on parchment, feeling very alone (2 Timothy 4:11). Many friends had fled the city. Fellow missionary Crescens had gone to Galatia while Titus went to Dalmatia. One companion, Demas, deserted him and the faith. One person even turned against Paul. Alexander the coppersmith did him "much harm," Paul lamented (4:14).

Paul's feelings poured out like tears in his letter. "Timothy, please come as soon as you can," Paul wrote (4:9), and he sealed his letter with a heartrending plea: "Do your best to get here before winter" (4:21)—before the north wind froze the earth and the chill of death overtook him.

Paul knew his time was short. As you can imagine at such tender moments, the apostle's thoughts roamed the corridors of his fondest memories. No friendship was dearer to Paul than his friendship with Timothy, who was pastoring the church at Ephesus, located in the region known today as Turkey.

Timothy had his work cut out for him in this bustling trade city, which was also the center of worship for the goddess Artemis. The trek from Ephesus to Rome would have required Timothy to travel by land and sea at least 840 miles. The distance gives new meaning to Paul asking Timothy to come soon and not wait. He was obviously lonely for him and knew it would take time to get to Rome.

Paul met Timothy on his second missionary journey. Their hearts linked together like teeth in gears. There was something about Timothy that drew them together, and they stayed close, so close that Paul refers to him as "my dear son" (2 Timothy 1:2). Endearing words.

No amount of reminiscing, however, removed Paul from the anguish of his circumstances. He was in a dungeon. He was, for the most part, alone. He was cold. Uncomfortable. No doubt in aching pain from former injuries. Yet, remarkably, Paul uttered not one complaint.

Soon Roman boots would be heard on the street above him, the death squad from the military barracks would be sent. Among them was the lictor carrying a long-handled axe, sharp as a razor. Little was spoken when soldiers came to collect a prisoner, whom they would place in chains and march through the streets so everyone would see that crime does not pay. Outside the walls of Rome, they would lead the condemned prisoner to Tre Fontane, where, tradition tells us, there was like a large stump. The body was bent over the stump. The lictor would lift the axe high and without a word, bring it down on the back of the neck of the victim, and the person's head would roll down into the dirt.

"The time of my death is near," Paul wrote, accepting his fate. He faced death not with dread but with hopeful anticipation of seeing His Savior (2 Timothy 4:6). He was at peace. He wrote to Timothy:

> *I have fought the good fight, I have finished the race, and I have remained faithful. And now the prize awaits me—the crown of righteousness, which the Lord, the righteous Judge, will give me on the day of his return. And the prize is not just for me but for all who eagerly look forward to his appearing.* (4:7–8)

Paul's faith had held true to the end, and he encouraged Timothy that his faith was just as genuine. Timothy's earliest mentors—his grandmother, Lois, and his mother, Eunice—had passed their faith to him, and Paul urged Timothy to cling tightly to the faith he had received. Timothy's father was Greek and, likely, an unbeliever (Acts 16:1–3).

I've always loved John Calvin's words regarding Timothy's mother, Eunice, as he writes, "When Timothy was an infant in her arms, Timothy sucked in righteousness along with his mother's milk." That's the most tender expression, and it's true. Eunice, who had gained faith from her mother, Lois, passed along to young Timothy the lullabies of Zion, the songs of the faith, the words of the Hebrew Scriptures.

The Impact of Mentors

May I pause here and give you time to think of your mother, if you were so blessed as Timothy. Or your father, if he was one of those men of God whose character you watched, whose words you heard, whose counsel you respected, whose warnings you heeded.

My mother was the earliest one to bring the name of Jesus to me. My father usually worked second shift in a machine shop, and he was rarely home for supper. It was my mother, older brother, older sister, and myself who were at the table. And, after we prayed, almost without exception, she would quote a verse of Scripture to us. She wrote it on little cards, and she handed the cards to each one of us and said, "I want you to memorize this." In fact, she said, "For every verse you memorize, I'll memorize two." I thought, *Hey, I'll do that.* So I memorized one. Sure enough, she memorized two. So I put her to the test and memorized two. She memorized four. I memorized a chapter. She memorized two chapters. I memorized James, and I strutted myself before her and quoted the book. She said, "Charles, sit down." She quoted Philippians and Colossians just like that. I said, "Game is over. I'm done!"

That was my mother. She certainly wasn't perfect, but she loved Jesus, and she made it clear that we were to know Jesus and walk with Him and learn His Word. To this day, there are verses I learned at our supper table I can still quote.

Maybe your home wasn't like mine. Many other things I could mention about my home might surprise you, but one thing was sure: God's Word was read and honored, respected and obeyed. Curse words were never allowed. Loud screaming at one another and arguments were never appropriate.

I remember my maternal grandfather as well. He meant more to me than any other adult male during my growing-up years. My father wasn't personal by temperament, and he rarely shared anything of an intimate nature with me. I know nothing of his father or mother. I know nothing of his place of birth. I know nothing of where he went to school. I only know that he had to quit school when his father died so his mother wouldn't starve, and he began to work for the railroad as an apprentice.

My maternal grandfather took an interest in me. Why? I can't tell you. But when my mom and dad and brother and sister and I would visit my place of birth, El Campo, Texas, I would enjoy seeing my grandfather, who was the township's justice of the peace.

He was known in the town of El Campo as L. O. Lundy, but I knew him as granddaddy, and I owe him so much. I love the way he lived his life. He wasn't one who paraded his faith. He lived his faith.

I've always appreciated the saying, "Give the gospel to others, and when necessary, use words." My grandfather could have said the same thing. He didn't preach to me. He lived the life. He loved me, and he showed it. He even had the courage to teach me how to drive!

I learned on a tractor near the little bay cottage my granddad owned, and I drove that tractor all over the field with my granddad right beside me, showing me how to do it. And then, he transferred me to his 1938 Ford. After we drove around the streets of El Campo when I was about 15 years old, he said to me, "Okay, little Charles, I want you to take this car into the garage."

I said, "Oh, granddaddy, I'm not sure."

"You can do it. Drive right on in," he said. He's sitting beside me, and I start driving in, and all of a sudden, *pow!* I hit the side of the garage and knocked off the right front fender. It was hanging off to the side, and he was just sitting there.

He said, "Why don't you back it up and try that again, son."

So I backed up, and I'm in tears. And I said, "Granddaddy, I can't do it."

He said, "Look, I can get new fenders, but I can't get new grandsons. Drive this car into that garage." So I did. I mistook the accelerator for the brake, which was why I got in the garage so quickly. But the second time, I realized the difference, and I drove it right in.

When Cynthia and I first married, we scraped together enough money, or so we thought, to make the payments on a home—about $60 per month for a $9,995 house. My granddaddy gave us $600 for the down payment, which was a whopping sum of money. I said, "Granddaddy, I will pay this back." He said, "No, that's a gift for you and your bride. I want you to be able to enjoy your new home a little more."

Was it your grandfather who mentored you? Was it an uncle or an aunt? Pause. Let's not rush through Paul's last letter. Let's think. Who was your first mentor? Maybe a pastor, quite likely a youth pastor?

A former youth pastor from another church held so much sway over our teenagers when we were at that church. His name was Eric Heard. Cynthia and I would say, "You know, if Eric says it, they'll believe it. If we say it, I'm not sure they get it, but when Eric says it, they do it." He was their youth pastor. Eric continued in that position for years, mentoring teenagers.

To this day, many adults in Southern California would tell you that Eric Heard was a mentor to them. Maybe a youth pastor was a mentor for you.

This is the time to thank God for your mentors. This is the time to remember them. Perhaps it was a neighbor who really loved you.

There was a man in our church named John. When he was a boy, he was abused. John told me that his father beat him with a leather strap, frequently. When John was in his early teenage years, his father lifted that horse strap to beat him again, and John grabbed him by the wrist and said to him, "You will not do that ever again!"

John pushed his dad aside, picked up a few of his belongings, got out on the road, and began to walk, leaving home and all the abuse and misery of that place of horrors. A distant neighbor saw John walking along with a little bag he was carrying. "John, where are you going?"

"I'm leaving home," John said.

"Come in. Come in, son," the neighbor said. He knew John's story, and he and his loving wife allowed John to live there, helping him as he grew up. When it came time for college, the man introduced John to Philadelphia College of Bible and helped him with his tuition. John graduated with honors and thought he was through. He was the best educated man in the entire family.

His friend said to him, "Oh no, no, now you're going on to seminary. You did so well at Philadelphia College of Bible, you need seminary training." And the man took John down to Dallas Theological Seminary. There, John went through the four-year Master of Theology program.

When John finished, he thought, "That's it." His friend said, "Oh no, no, you're doctoral material and you're going to stay on." He helped John with his tuition, and he earned his doctorate. We know him today as Dr. John Hannah, a longtime, beloved professor who was the chair of the historical theology department as a faculty member at DTS for many, many years.

Few people knew about John's background because mentors aren't well known. Often those they mentor become well known.

The "Paul" in My Life

When I was deployed as a Marine to the island of Okinawa after being married for less than two years, I was 8,000 miles from home and lonely. I couldn't be farther from family and from my dear wife, whom I desperately missed. It was during this time I met

Bob Newkirk who was the representative from The
Navigators, ministering to the Marines on the island.

We were like Paul and Timothy. Our hearts were
linked from almost the first evening we met. Bob got
me involved in the topical memory system. To pass the
course, I had to recite all 168 verses, with each verse's
reference before and after it, in one sitting. I remember
doing that, and when I finished, we were sitting in Bob's
car on the slope of a hill. I'd been there several months.
Bob had tears in his eyes, and he said to me, "Well done,
man. Now you're just getting started."

He introduced me to an in-depth, advanced
Bible-study method that we began to do together. Talk
about a mentor, talk about helping a young, lonely
Marine, an eternity from home, not able to be with my
wife or family!

Time went on and he got me involved in leading
some Christian meetings he had started. It was called
"GIs for Christ." My mentor would stand in the back of
the room while I led the meetings. I would teach.
I would sometimes sing. I was involved in leadership—
one of the first times I'd ever been a leader.

As we were going back to the base near the time of my departure from the island, I said to him, "Bob, I think I may be going into the ministry. I never thought of it before." Now, tears were in my eyes.

He said, "Well, of course, you're a natural." I thought, *Natural?* I didn't know what natural meant.

He said, "Oh, Chuck, you've got it."

I said, "No, I don't. Maybe it's some kind of gift God's given me, but Bob, I have a long way to go, and I need to be trained for this. I'm not really qualified to enter Dallas Theological Seminary"—the school I wanted to attend.

He said, "Well, I'm going to pray you in. I'm going to believe God will get you into that place."

When I came home, I told Cynthia all about it. She was thrilled. She had always wanted to marry a minister.

We went to DTS together, and I was interviewed. Bob's prayers were answered, and I was allowed to come in on probation. Boy, that was fabulous! I became the lawn boy on campus, earning 75 cents an hour and all you could eat. It was wonderful! I remember thinking, *How blessed am I? Thanks, Bob, for your prayers.*

Timothy must have thought the same thing when he got that letter from Paul—*Thanks, Paul, for calling me your dear son.*

Who Was Your Mentor?

Think about it. Who was your mentor? Mom, dad, grandparent, neighbor, or a friend you met along the way? Maybe a pastor or youth pastor? You're different today because of the time that person spent with you.

Timothy grew to the point where he was able to pastor the church in Ephesus. Paul wrote to him,

> *Timothy, my dear son, be strong through the grace that God gives you in Christ Jesus. You have heard me teach things that have been confirmed by many reliable witnesses. Now teach these truths to other trustworthy people who will be able to pass them on to others.* (2 Timothy 2:1–2)

The *you* is Timothy. *Me* is Paul. "The things you, Timothy, learned from me as we sat around the campfire, as we walked together, as we sailed the seas together, as we traveled those miles together, as we went through suffering together . . . the things you learned from me, pass along to trustworthy people who will be able to teach others also." It's a ministry of multiplication.

Who Are You Mentoring?

A little over a year ago, I said to Cynthia, "Here we are at this age, with not only four children, but 10 grandchildren. I'm going to pick a couple of our grandsons and start spending special time with them."

I share this with you only to give you grandparents an idea. You can't miss as a grandparent. You foul up as a parent, but when it comes to grandparenting, boy, they think you hung the moon.

Just meet with them. I'm meeting with two of my grandsons. We share with each other the cracks in our lives, the great days, the hard days, the beautiful experiences, the mistakes we've made. We open the vault of our inner chambers, and we let out the secrets with one another.

It's all done confidentially upstairs in my study, surrounded by my books, sitting on a sofa and comfortable chairs, and we quietly review life together.

There's no agenda. Oh, we're using a couple of the books I've written as a sort of guide, but that leads us into the discussion of whatever's on their heart. Both are employed. Neither of them is married. Both are in their 30s and both are outstanding young men. They'll make great husbands and great fathers. They hang on every word, not only from me, but now from one another. I notice, as I sit and listen, as the two of them are blending together—as the chemistry is growing between them. I had never thought about that before, but when you mentor others, those who are being mentored end up growing together.

You want to know something? This is going to surprise you. If you're an older adult who has grown up in the church, you know more biblical truth than most people younger than you. You do. You have heard books of the Bible explained. You have heard stories about characters of the Bible unfolded for you. You have listened as doctrines have been preached. You've had your Bible open in your lap. You've taken notes. You remember things that were said about the men and women in Scripture. You've learned things about Matthew and Mark, Luke and John, and Jesus' ministry to the disciples.

Have you shared that with anyone else? Who are you mentoring?

You say, "Well, I'm not a minister." Well, that's in your favor, believe me. When they find out you're a minister, they sort of put you on a pedestal. But when you're one of them, there's no pedestal. They'll really listen. They really want to know. They want to have your help in dealing with life.

You know what young people struggle with? Of course you do. Lust, temptation, impatience, and the list goes on. Like how to have a date life that doesn't leave you feeling guilty. We talk openly about that. We talk openly about finances, how to handle your money, how to do a good job at work, how to put in a solid eight to ten hours a day. We talk about life as we live it. We discuss the mistakes we've made, the struggles we've had, and we talk about marriage and about parenting.

Most men enter the world of fatherhood having given very little thought to what's involved. There's no handbook, so a mentor takes the place of a handbook.

For you women, think of what it would mean to a younger girl to hear about motherhood or about what to look for in a husband. Or, if she's called to be single, what's involved in living the single life to the glory of God.

Long before I met Cynthia, she, too, already had a heart for missions gained from the mentorship of her beloved mother Laverne Parker, who died of cancer at age 46. In her short life, she had been a godly influence to Cynthia.

Before I met Cynthia, I'd never known a young lady more interested in spiritual things. I thank her mother for that. And her mother loved me as much, if not more, than my own mother loved me. She saw a future for me that my mother never saw. I found a home in their family closer than I found in my own family, and her mother was the secret.

When their house burned to the ground, they lived a mile from her maternal grandparents Mamie and Marvin Hood. Cynthia, at four years old, ran that mile to tell them their house was burning to the ground. They moved in with her grandparents. Granny Hood was an invalid, and Cynthia watched her mother nurse her grandmother, faithfully taking care of her needs. To this day, she will tell you the story of what that meant to her as a little girl growing up in the home of Pawpaw and Granny Hood.

Passing the Faith to the Next Generation ▬▬▬

I can't convey this more sincerely than I am now: you need to be a mentor for someone else. This world is dying on the vine. People are wondering who will help them find their way.

Jim Elliot wrote it this way, "Wherever you are, be all there. Live to the hilt every situation you believe to be the will of God." Paul, though in a dungeon, was "all there" when he wrote Timothy in Ephesus. I want to believe that Timothy made it to Rome, traveling those 800-plus miles to see his mentor one last time.

I believe he brought with him John Mark and the books and the parchments and the cloak. Can you imagine these four men huddled together, Dr. Luke, Paul, Timothy, and John Mark, singing together and praying together in the dungeon? Can you imagine the strength their visit brought Paul after they had been with him? Can you imagine their renewed vision after being with Paul? Passing along hope and encouragement is what a mentor does for those he or she helps. Mentors endear themselves to those they mentor.

My life is completely different because of those who mentored me. I had seventeen mentors who were my professors at DTS when I was a student. I could name every one of them. They were faculty members who took an interest in me, even though I was accepted into the school on probation. They treated me just like any other student. We had wonderful times together. I can still quote their words I heard during my four years at that great school.

Mentors. They change your life. Think about it. Think about not only your mentors, but whom you are mentoring. "Wherever you are, be all there." Immerse yourself in the life of another person younger than you. You will never, ever regret it.

Jesus Christ mentored twelve men. They're called His disciples. I was talking with the two men I'm mentoring, and I said to them, "Have you ever thought about Jesus with His disciples?" They rested together. They traveled together. They ate together. I don't know where they got their food. I don't know how they got their clothing. Someone provided it for them. I don't know how they took care of their families. They had no insurance policy.

They had no retirement program. Jesus just said, "Follow Me." They were all there. One failed, Judas, but the other eleven turned the world upside down, having been mentored by the Savior.

They quoted Him. They worshiped Him. They loved Him until the day of their death—most of them dying as martyrs for His sake. They were "all there" because Jesus cared enough to pour His life into those few men. He could have chosen 20, 30, 1,200. But He chose a small group and committed Himself to them, and they were never the same.

Times are not getting easier. They're getting harder. Enduring is all part of the Christian life. If you don't know Christ, that's step one for you. Turn your life over to Him, come to the foot of the cross, acknowledge the fact that you're a sinner and you need a Savior. Your life is a mess, and you've made it that way. Come to Christ like you are, and He'll take you and change you into what He would like you to be. You will be a different person after giving your life to Christ. When you do that, be "all there" in a mentoring relationship with another person, grow in faith . . . and live life to the hilt!

Dear Father, thank You for those who cared enough about us to spend hours with us over the years. Thank You for their lives and what they mean to us. For our parents and grandparents, for neighbors and friends and youth workers and pastors, teachers, those who loved us long before we knew our way around. How grateful we are, Father, for Your raising up of individuals who change our lives by Your grace. May You find us faithful, I pray, as we become mentors to those around us. In the name of Christ, I ask this. Amen.

CHAPTER 2

Look Within
Can You Endure Hardship?

Delivered September 29, 2024

Endure suffering along with me, as a good soldier of Christ Jesus. Soldiers don't get tied up in the affairs of civilian life, for then they cannot please the officer who enlisted them. And athletes cannot win the prize unless they follow the rules. And hardworking farmers should be the first to enjoy the fruit of their labor. Think about what I am saying. The Lord will help you understand all these things.

2 TIMOTHY 2:3–7

The World War II generation is known as the greatest for a reason. Then, as a nation, we willingly rationed, and we sacrificed. We put a decal of a star on our window that patriotically announced our son or our daughter was serving our country. If the star was removed and a cross took its place, neighborhoods grieved the loss of one of their own, and we pressed on.

As a child, I knew that our nation was at war in Europe and in the Pacific—both sides of our country. We lived near the Gulf Coast, and so we had blackouts. I often went to bed at night wondering, *Will we be invaded tonight?* Our dads worked double shifts. Even our moms worked when it wasn't popular for women to work.

Oh, I know, I'm reminiscing. But the Greatest Generation exhibited a quality we all need today. They *endured*. Walk among the crosses at Normandy, and you cannot hold back the tears. There's something about battle sites that still put a lump in my throat and call to me to persevere through pain.

Paul, in a dungeon in Rome, wrote to Timothy pastoring the church in Ephesus more than 800 miles away. Paul endured, and he challenged Timothy to endure with him. He told him in his letter, "Timothy, it's your temperament to be a little timid, a little reluctant, a little soft. You can easily drift. Timothy, stand firm."

When our class graduated from Dallas Theological Seminary, the president of the school, John F. Walvoord, addressed us at the baccalaureate service. He made a statement I'll never forget. "I fear that we may be graduating men with too many beliefs but not enough convictions."

I've thought about that over the 60-plus years of my ministry. Am I a man of just beliefs, or do I have some steel in my bones? In a group that blasphemes the name of Christ, would I say nothing, so they'll like me? Would I rather be liked than right? Would you?

I've gone through a lot of pain in the last year—more than I can remember in my life. By the grace of God, I had been healthy and strong and able to get around and move without the help of a cane. Suddenly that changed. Am I still strong within? Am I still willing to bear the toil, endure the pain, supported by His Word?

Dr. Walvoord is gone, as are all of those who taught me. Their words are lingering memories. Many of those from the Greatest Generation, my parents included, are no longer living. Cynthia's parents included. The secret is not to try to live back then. It's to live in the present. I know that. But, now just as then, we must endure through pain. Do we know that?

In her classic poem, "Guests," Martha Snell Nicholson described what it's like to live with pain.

> Pain knocked upon my door and said
> That she had come to stay;
> And though I would not welcome her
> But bade her go away,
>
> She entered in. Like my own shade
> She followed after me,
> And from her stabbing, stinging sword
> No moment was I free.
>
> And then one day, another knocked
> Most gently at my door.
> I cried, "No, Pain is living here,
> There is not room for more."
>
> And then I heard His tender voice,
> "'Tis I, be not afraid."
> And from the day He entered in—
> The difference it made![1]

Enduring Pain with Christ

Paul assured Timothy, "Endure hardship, endure pain. Christ is right there." Even the all-powerful Son of God enrolled Himself in the school of suffering:

Even though Jesus was God's Son, he learned obedience from the things he suffered. In this way, God qualified him as a perfect High Priest, and he became the source of eternal salvation for all those who obey him. (Hebrews 5:8–9)

Seven hundred years before Jesus was born, Isaiah prophesied that He would be "a man of sorrows, acquainted with deepest grief" (Isaiah 53:3). You want the ultimate picture of enduring? Look at the crucifixion. While nailed to a cross with iron stakes, out of Jesus' mouth came no cursing, no retaliatory words, only "Father, forgive them, for they don't know what they are doing" (Luke 23:34). He endured the pain.

Physical pain has been my companion lately, as never before. But not pain like many have suffered. Mine was minor compared to some I know, but mine was major compared to my past. Hours of solitude. Too painful to lean back, too painful to lift a leg. After being in the hospital for some time, I almost had to learn to walk again.

I'd never known that experience. "Endure pain, Chuck," Paul might have told me. But enduring physical pain is a rather simple accomplishment compared to what Paul was referring to. He was talking about enduring the pain of persecution.

We must become the models of what Christ requires of His followers. We must be soldiers of the cross, followers of the Lamb, unafraid to own His cause, people who don't blush to speak His name.

Your children will be in classes where the professor will take delight in trying to destroy their faith. Do they know how to defend it? Do they run the risk of speaking up even if doing so makes a difference in their grade? A lot depends on what you have taught them. In a place where groupthink is so powerful, are they able to stand alone and say no?

Illustrations of Endurance

Paul illustrated endurance using three inspiring examples—soldiers, athletes, and farmers:

> *Soldiers don't get tied up in the affairs of civilian life, for then they cannot please the officer who enlisted them. And athletes cannot win the prize unless they follow the rules. And hardworking farmers should be the first to enjoy the fruit of their labor.* (2 Timothy 2:4–6)

Be like a Disciplined Soldier

A soldier is known for one thing: discipline. Without discipline, the battle is not won, the hill is not taken, the enemy is not defeated. Victory requires tough discipline.

I remember standing inspection in the Marine Corps, and the man next to me was being grilled by the drill instructor. He stood about three inches from the young man's face and unloaded on him, using harassment to break him down. The new recruit next to me stood straight and strong as the drill instructor said to him, "Why in the world did you volunteer for this outfit anyway?"

His answer was superb. He said, "Sir, I need the discipline, sir."

For once I saw a drill instructor without words. Next, he came in front of me, and what he said to me is none of your business! Every one of us recruits went through that kind of harassment, every one of us. Why? To get the discipline going.

We showed up as a bunch of ragtag rookies who needed, in a matter of weeks, to be trained into a combat force that could make an amphibious landing or could carry heavy packs or could run in heavy boots or could sacrifice or could drag their wounded buddies off the field without hesitation.

I recently read that every branch of the service is having trouble getting its quota of enlistments. Who wants to join up for something that rugged? Have you wondered, *What if we were suddenly at war? Who would fight? Who would be the warriors?*

Paul could have used any analogy, but he used a soldier, referring to the discipline, the mind-set, and the actions of one who has been trained to follow orders against all odds. Soldiers step into battle knowing that, even if outnumbered, they will take the objective.

The man who mentored me, Bob Newkirk, was among the Greatest Generation. He said to me that most of the young men in his high school graduating class went directly to the enlistment center and wrote their names on the line which their parents signed for them as they joined the forces of the military. That is how the war was won.

Like a soldier, a good soldier, stand firm for your faith, men and women. This is a wicked world. This culture is moving in the wrong direction, and you know it. It will take steel in your spiritual bones to take a stand. Take it, like a good soldier.

"Timothy, don't yield. Be different," Paul urged. Over and over, Paul wrote in his letter, "But you." "The world is such and such . . . *but you.*" "People want to hear what they want to hear . . . *but you.*" The emphasis is on, "You be different, Timothy." If anyone is going to tell the truth, make sure the pastor in Ephesus speaks the truth like a good soldier.

Be like a Devoted Athlete

Paul didn't stop there. His next analogy refers to an athlete. Talk about devotion! Picture the athletes at the Olympics. Competing in the Olympics is the rewarding part. The rugged part takes place month after month after month after month after month of devoted training where athletes get up early to train. Many of them move from the comfort of their home to the place where their particular coach teaches and trains. Some leave school that they might devote themselves to training for an event—running, swimming, wrestling, boxing, or whatever event is their specialty.

Devoted athletes are sleek and fit, willing to sweat and fight through muscle pain as they ache through the day, through the night, until the event. In the days of Paul, those who ran in the Olympiad swore to Zeus, the god of many of those countries, that they would devote at least ten consecutive months to training. If they broke their word, they would be disqualified and sometimes scourged. "Toughen up, get at it, stay at it!" That's what this passage is teaching. This isn't a calm little soft pillow to drop onto at night. This is a sinewy letter. It's got muscles.

I remember several years ago, Cynthia and I were living in the Los Angeles area, and there was a track nearby. It was a perfect place to work out. We would go there early in the morning together, and we'd jog. It was a marvelous place to stay fit and to stay with our program of training.

One morning, very early, she had to get to Insight for Living for her work. I said, "I think I'm going to go on alone." I'd forgotten that this track that early in the morning was used by a number of the Olympian athletes who were going to be running in the Los Angeles Olympic Games. I got there, and I saw them. So I backed out of the gate like, I don't want anybody to see me here.

One of them recognized me!

"Chuck, come in. Come on in," he called. He was one of the men training for the decathlon, and he said, "You can train with us."

I backed away, "Oh, no, no, no. Really, you're joking."

He motioned and said, "Wait." Then he walked over to me and shook my hand. He was very kind, and he said, "Why don't you and I run together?"

I said, "No, come on, man. I'll crawl compared to you."

"I promise I will not try to show you up. You set the pace," he replied. "I'll keep whatever pace you set."

"Okay, good." So, I began to walk, and he walked, and we walked along together. He was laughing and we were talking. It's hard to talk and jog, but I began to jog, and he kept talking, and I talked less, because I needed to save my breath because I knew I would die at any moment! Then I'm thinking, *I'm going to kick us up a notch*. So I did, and before long I'm running full bore. I'm not going to tell you how fast it was, but it was pathetic!

He kept pace right there with me and hardly broke a sweat, still talking, still laughing with me.

Then, I noticed when I looked over, he was running backwards!

He said, "I have to keep these muscles (and he named them here in the front) in good shape." He said, "Go on ahead."

I replied, panting, "Well, I'm about through." So I sat up in the bleachers and watched them for a little while longer. *They were athletes.* They stayed at it. I mean, what he did with me was nothing compared to the exercises they did—the relays they ran, the sprints. They ran like a flash! The harmony and the cooperation, the *esprit de corps*, among them was wonderful to watch. All of them fit. They were training for the games. They were *devoted.*

I served on the board of the corporate members of Dallas Theological Seminary for several years. I loved it because I could sit next to my mentor, Ray Stedman, who had been a board member for some time, and other men I admired and loved to be with. I especially enjoyed being on the board with Tom Landry, coach of the Dallas Cowboys football team. That was back in the days when the Cowboys were doing things they rarely do now—they were winning!

When we would break for lunch, Coach Landry's table would just instantly fill up. On one occasion, I made it to his side and had a chance to talk briefly with him. I said, "Coach, how in the world have you won so many games?" His team made it to the playoffs 18 out of 29 seasons. I said, "How do you do it?" Always modest, always understated, Coach Landry was the kind of individual who, the better you got to know him, the more you respected him.

He said with a little smile, "Well, Chuck," he said, "I guess you could say we just had better athletes."

I said, "No, there has to be more than that. Come on."

He said, "Well, let me put it this way. My job as a coach is to train athletes to do with all their hearts what they hate, so that they might accomplish what they've wanted all their lives."

It's called *devotion*.

It was my privilege to help lead Mr. Landry's memorial service at the Meyerson Center. The best part was being behind the scenes and walking among the giants, the football players I'd seen only on television, as they thought about what they would say when they took the microphone to honor their hero. Many of them referred to him as the father they never had. They spoke through tears about the one who had trained them to do what they hated but who led them to accomplish what they had always wanted.

Paul said to Timothy, "I may not be at your side right now, but stay devoted. Don't drift. Don't wander. Be a man of prayer. Pray daily."

Howard Taylor wrote the biography of his father, Hudson Taylor, the founder of China Inland Mission. Cynthia and I read the two-volume work by Howard Taylor during seminary. It's magnificent. The son said of his father, "The sun never rose for 40 years in China but that God did not find my father on his knees in prayer." Devotion, discipline, staying at it. Don't get soft. Our times are soft, but our times don't dictate to us. Stay with that journal. Keep up that walk with the Lord.

Jim Elliot put it beautifully, "God is on His throne and we're on His footstool, and there's only a knee's distance in between." Stay on your knees.

Pray for your children. Pray for them to stand alone, stand firm, and endure. Pray that they will endure in a marriage when things get tough, endure in a job when it isn't pleasant, endure in a crowd that mocks them or in a class at school where the other students poke fun at them. Tell them what an honor that is. Tell them the stories from your own life.

Be like a Diligent Farmer

There's another analogy in the passage. "Like a hardworking farmer." I love the way Paul puts it. Not just a farmer, but a hardworking farmer. If there's one word I'd use to describe farmers it's *diligence*. Diligence. Farmers work from morning till night, whether it's dairy farming or orchard farming or crop farming. Pulling the stumps, plowing the fields, fertilizing the soil, planting the crops, pruning, fighting insects, and then harvest time comes.

It was my privilege years ago to preach in a farming community in the San Joaquin Valley, California. I stayed in the home of a farmer and his wife. His crop happened to be oranges. I'm telling you, the fragrance of those oranges was intoxicating.

Early one morning I stepped outside his farmhouse, and he went with me. His hands were so calloused, you could strike a match on them.

I commented, "Boy, look at this orchard." Acres and acres of orange trees stretched before us. It was harvest time, and the limbs were hanging low. I reached up and plucked one off.

"Look at that," I said. "To think that that just happened."

He said, "Give me that!" He jerked the orange out of my hand and stuck it before my nose and said, "_That did not just happen!_"

And then he went through the process of telling me what he'd been through to grow a crop of oranges like the one I'd plucked. I got tired just listening to him!

When I drive by farms that are this beautiful, I just roll up my window and keep on driving. No thanks! It's work! Never-ending work!

Diligence.

If you were looking for the easy way, why in the world did you trust in Christ? Last time I checked, this Man of Sorrows knows grief and pain like few have ever known. What we love about Him is His endurance.

Never fickle, never self-serving, always at it. And by age 33 or so, He prayed to the Father, "I've done what You sent Me to do. Mission accomplished." Then He went to the cross. I love Him for that. I serve a Savior who endured. He never backed away. He never gave up.

An Inspiring Model ═══════════

Amy Carmichael decided not to give in to her day. Though frail and given to illness, she attended a Keswick conference away from her homeland of Ireland. She listened to great men, like Hudson Taylor, speak, and she was stirred in her spirit. She determined, "I must go."

Through the giving of faithful donors and her own savings, she took a ship all the way from her homeland to southern India. She got off the ship and started from scratch. She began to rescue girls caught in sex trafficking, living debauched, broken, shameful lives, and unable to get out of it. She made it possible for them to return to dignity and life, and she endeared herself to them, one after another by the hundreds.

So modest, Amy wouldn't even put her name on the early books she wrote. You can still find them in bookstores, but don't think they're bedside reading. You'll need to think deeply, because she wrote deeply. She lived deeply. Never married. Toward the end, she worked from her sick bed. I love her works. They're right next to my elbow in my study. I often pull one from the shelf and read it aloud.

In her poem, "Make Me Thy Fuel, O Flame of God," she expresses her devotion to the Lord.

> From prayer that asks that I may be
> Sheltered from winds that beat on Thee,
> From fearing when I should aspire,
> From faltering when I should climb higher,
> From silken self, O Captain, free
> Thy soldier who would follow Thee. . . .
>
> Give me the love that leads the way,
> The faith that nothing can dismay,
> The hope no disappointments tire,
> The passion that will burn like fire,
> Let me not sink to be a clod:
> Make me Thy fuel, Flame of God.[2]

That's endurance. Let's be numbered among people like her. Let's not be ashamed or afraid. Hard times call for tough-minded people who have soft hearts but thick skin. Or, as I read recently, "The heart of a lamb with the hide of a rhinoceros."

May we be people who are known by our endurance, who, in our walk with Christ, exhibit the discipline of a soldier, the devotion of an athlete, and the diligence of a farmer.

*Help us, our Father, to be soldiers of the
cross, followers of the Lamb. May we
anticipate heaven and all that You have for
us, but before then, may we live for You with
our whole heart enduring the pain.
For Jesus' sake. Amen.*

CHAPTER 3

Look Around
Do You Stand Firm?

Delivered October 6, 2024

*You should know this, Timothy,
that in the last days there will be very difficult times. . . .
But you must remain faithful to the things you have
been taught. You know they are true, for you know
you can trust those who taught you.*

2 TIMOTHY 3:1, 14

Martin Luther had no patience with those who made trouble in the church. He had a special description for them: "boars in God's vineyard."

Troublemakers break our hearts. They tear up what is beautiful and good about the church. When I was in seminary, my professor, Dr. Howard Hendricks, also had a great saying about them. "Never forget, men," he said, "where there is light, there are bugs." We laughed then, but a few years later we weren't laughing.

Bugs in the church drive you *crazy*. Some of them are just a nuisance. Some are like swarms that come in groups, that work together making life miserable for you. Some sting and bite. A few are poisonous and spread the diseases of heresy and dissension. These human bugs, as we refer to them, are nothing new. They go back not only to the days of Martin Luther but also to the days of Paul and even further.

There have always been those who made life miserable for leaders. Joshua had to deal with Achan, whose sin brought about defeat on the battlefield and death in the camp. David had to deal with Nabal—the scrooge who wouldn't share a few sheep from his massive flock in appreciation for David's protection. Later, David had to deal with Shimei, who threw rocks at him when he was retreating from the throne, having abdicated it to his son, Absalom.

Elisha's own servant, Gehazi, deceived him. Paul was harassed by Alexander the coppersmith, who, in Paul's words, "fought against everything we said" (2 Timothy 4:15). He warned Timothy, "He's still around and he'll make trouble for you too!"

In his third epistle, John mentioned Diotrephes, the church boss who loved "to be first" and hurled accusations at John "with malicious words" (3 John 1:9–10 NASB). John said that, if he came, he would "call attention to his deeds" (1:10 NASB). The two things that troublemakers don't like are confrontation and exposure, and that's so hard to do with difficult people who are tough to deal with.

Living in Difficult Times

I have a friend who has a ministry online, and he works with pastors who are at the end of their rope. They're wounded. They're discouraged. Some are disillusioned. Some have quit. Many of them are like that because they've lost the battle with troublemakers. My friend's ministry gives them hope and reassurance.

I love to preach sermons about grace and joy, hope and happiness. But when I come across passages like 2 Timothy 3, there's nothing to laugh about. Paul wrote to Timothy to open his eyes: "Timothy, don't walk around in a dream world." He warned his younger protégé, "You may want things to be beautiful and lovely and right, but these troublemakers are none of the above."

Paul's words to Timothy flash like red lights on our dashboard:

> *You should know this, Timothy, that in the*
> *last days there will be very difficult times.*
> (2 Timothy 3:1)

Some think of the "last days" as a time in the future, the last part of the great tribulation. In fact, the last days cover the centuries from the time Christ came until the time Christ will return. It's *all* the last days.

Things are getting worse, and they will continue to get worse. Paul used the Greek word, *chalepos*, translated "difficult." The term appears only one other time in the New Testament, in Matthew. Matthew used it to describe the two demon-filled men who lived in the tombs. By the power of demonic forces, they broke the chains that had bound them and terrorized the community. Matthew called them *chalepos*—"extremely violent" (Matthew 8:28 NASB). They were dangerous! Paul was warning Timothy that "terrorizing times will come— harsh, hard to deal with, dangerous times."

One of my mentors translated it like this: "*savage* times will come." Are we living in these times? Have they come? Anyone who keeps his or her eyes and ears open to what's happening in the world would agree they have—even in our churches.

Perhaps you've experienced a church that has begun to drift. You're heartbroken because it once was a lighthouse, a citadel of truth. No longer. They bought into unbiblical teaching. They listened to the world and decided to move in step with it.

Paul wrote Timothy and all church leaders through the centuries: "Open your eyes. You're living in treacherous, savage times!" Paul wasn't saying that leaders should become negative or that they should be fighters. Rather, he was saying that they shouldn't run from a fight. They shouldn't sit back and let the sheep be attacked, taken advantage of, or mistreated. That's not a good shepherd. That's a weak shepherd. Everyone wants to be liked, but we must pay more attention to being right than to being liked. Being a strong leader in difficult times means you deal with what is wrong and rejoice over what is right. You encourage the latter, but you confront the former.

How to Spot a Troublemaker

To help us spot troublemakers in the church, Paul listed their characteristics. I think of Paul's description as an autopsy of depravity. He sliced open humanity's fallen nature, laid out all the parts, and revealed the wrongdoings of those who make the church miserable. He wrote,

> *For people will be lovers of self, lovers of money, boastful, arrogant, slanderers, disobedient to parents, ungrateful, unholy, unloving, irreconcilable, malicious gossips, without self-control, brutal, haters of good, treacherous, reckless, conceited, lovers of pleasure rather than lovers of God, holding to a form of godliness although they have denied its power; avoid such people as these.* (2 Timothy 3:2–5 NASB)

Let's look closer at these characteristics that come together to make a detailed portrait of the troublemakers we might encounter in our church.

Lovers of Self

First, Paul said they would be "lovers of self"
(2 Timothy 3:2 NASB). Self-lovers are narcissistic. In
their view, they are the most important people on earth.
A narcissistic husband can make his wife miserable.
A narcissistic wife and mother can ruin a family. A
narcissistic person can ruin fellowship in a church.
"Watch out for them," Paul warned Timothy . . . and us.

Lovers of Money

They would also be "lovers of money" (2 Timothy 3:2
NASB). These people see money and possessions as their
means of security and significance. They find their worth
in their money, not in their strong, righteous character.
They also use money to get their way. That's why I often
tell young pastors to pay no attention to who gives what
in their church. Stay out of the offering. That's the work
of ushers, elders, and those who deal with finances. Let
them do their work with integrity. Don't take money in
front of the church. Don't take money in an aisle. Don't
handle people's money. I have never known the names
of the givers in the churches I've served nor the amounts
they gave. Giving has no effect on my treatment of

individuals, and it never will. Lovers of money want to manipulate others with their money, and they seek greater influence because they have money. "Watch out for materialists like these, Timothy," Paul said. And the same applies to us.

Boastful

The third characteristic is boastfulness (2 Timothy 3:2 NASB). The boastful person isn't afraid to brag about his or her own significance and importance. Paul's Greek word for "boastful" pictured ancient vagabonds who traveled from town to town, making great promises, collecting money from people, and then disappearing. Later, they bragged about how they fleeced people. We've all encountered boastful charlatans.

Arrogant

The next characteristic is arrogance (2 Timothy 3:2 NASB). Is there anything more difficult to deal with than an arrogant individual? This is a person who lords it over people. Paul's choice of Greek word has two parts, *hyper* and *ephanos*. *Hyper* is the word for "above" and *ephanos* means "to appear." These people like to appear above others as they look down their noses at everyone else. Be careful about putting arrogant individuals in charge. Look for humble people and avoid arrogant ones.

Revilers

Paul then warned about "revilers" (2 Timothy 3:2 NASB 1995). The Greek term is *blasphemos*. We get our word *blasphemy* from it. These people slander others, put other people down, say false things about them, and treat them with contempt. Even worse, they blaspheme the living God when they treat Him that way.

Disobedient to Parents

Paul adds to his list, disobedience to parents (2 Timothy 3:2). In their homes growing up, they fought to get their way. They made trouble for their parents, for their teachers at school, and for the police officer on the corner. These troublemakers aren't hard to spot. They are the ones who refuse to cooperate with anyone in authority.

Ungrateful, Unholy, Unloving

Paul's next three characteristics of troublemakers begin with the letters U-N. Ungrateful people lack a thankful spirit. They see themselves as being entitled. They're not thankful for what they have, and they always want more. Unholy people lack appreciation for and reverence for what is sacred. Unloving people think only of themselves and show no interest in caring for the needs of others.

Irreconcilable

Another type of troublemaker in the church is one who is unwilling to settle differences. They are "irreconcilable" (2 Timothy 3:3 NASB). They hold a grudge. They are unable to work through issues. They know nothing of the meaning of negotiating, giving-and-taking, cooperating in a group, or even admitting when they are wrong. Irreconcilable people are unforgiving people. Guard against becoming friends with these kinds of people.

Malicious Gossips

Paul also warns against "malicious gossips" (2 Timothy 3:3 NASB). Has anything wounded more people than the vice of gossip? People who spread false rumors are often genuinely unaware of the damage they have caused. They're so used to gossiping, they don't even think about the hurt it brings to the other person. They care little about what is accurate or what is confidential or whether they can prove what they are saying. Here's a little advice: before you pass along information, be certain you have the facts straight. And if it's about another person, ask permission to share it before you tell it. Otherwise, keep it to yourself.

No Self-Control

The next characteristic is that troublemakers have "no self-control" (2 Timothy 3:3 NASB). These are people who are unable to tap the brakes. "Loose living" describes their lifestyle. They are frequently loose sexually, loose verbally, loose ethically. "No self-control" is a dangerous way to live because this free-wheeling lifestyle hurts so many people. Keep these morally unrestrained people away from leadership in the church.

Brutal

Paul warned that troublemakers can be "brutal" (2 Timothy 3:3 NASB)—which is an accurate word to describe a bully. Bullies are not only in schools; they're also in churches. Even some pastors become bullies.

Given authority to lead a church, they set the pace and set the vision, and before long they start believing their own stuff. They do not listen well to others, and they lack gentleness and compassion. They rough up anyone who questions them. The Greek word for "brutal" was sometimes used for wild animals, especially for lions—which is, tragically, a good description of pastors who become bullies in the pulpit.

Haters of Good

There are those who purposely choose *not* to do what is right, perhaps because doing right is difficult to pull off. "Haters of good" (2 Timothy 3:3 NASB) will go with the flow. They will pay attention to the opinions of others rather than the truth of the Scriptures.

Treacherous

According to Paul, troublemakers will also be "treacherous" (2 Timothy 3:4 NASB). The Greek word means, basically, "to turn over." It was the word used to describe Judas, who turned over Jesus to the mob when they came to arrest Him in the garden. Remember how Judas did it? With a kiss. How deceitful, how treacherous!

Now realize, Judas was exposed to all the same truths, miracles, and teachings from Christ that the other eleven disciples were exposed to . . . but none of it stopped his treachery. He was a traitor at heart. He may have looked like the other disciples, but he was not like them at all. So skillfully did he hide his true nature that the others trusted him with the money box. Later, John saw Judas for who he was. John wrote bluntly, "He was a thief" (John 12:6).

Treachery is one thing you cannot tolerate among staff members. They need to pull together, work together, deal in truth, be vulnerable, open, and honest. Watch out for those who turn against you when you're not watching. Jesus faced the mob and finally was arrested because of Judas—who later hanged himself when he realized too late that he had done wrong. Isn't it interesting, no one today ever names a son Judas? Even the name has a "hiss" to it.

Reckless

The next characteristic is recklessness (2 Timothy 3:4 NASB), which, in Greek, implies falling forward and being unable to stop. Reckless people fall quickly and are suddenly on the floor before they realize it! These individuals push their way into things and are unable to stop themselves.

Conceited

The Greek word for "conceited" (2 Timothy 3:4 NASB) literally means "wrapped in smoke." Conceited people are always "blowing smoke," as we would say. They see themselves as smarter and better than others. They do not make good team members because it's never about anyone else but themselves.

Lovers of Pleasure Rather than Lovers of God

According to Paul, troublemakers "love pleasure rather than God" (2 Timothy 3:4 NASB). This is where churches can often get off target. Church leaders start appealing to the desires and opinions of individuals who want to feel good. God is never obligated to make us feel good. His goal in life is not to give us what we want but what we need. People who seek pleasure instead of God forget that.

Holding to a Form of Godliness

Finally, Paul warns us that troublemakers will hold to "a form of godliness" (2 Timothy 3:5). This is raw hypocrisy. Jesus reserved His strongest rebukes for hypocrites. The Greek word, *hypokrites*, refers to actors on the stage playing a part. It's the word for "wearing a mask." For these troublemakers, their religion is all show. Beneath their mask of piety, they have no power to be godly because they have rejected God.

One of the best things you can do as you grow up in Christ is to get rid of the mask. People love it when you're authentic, when you're vulnerable, when you don't know and you're able to say, "I don't know."

When you don't deserve the credit, say, "I get no credit for that. She's the one who carried this out." Or, "He's the one who's better at it than I am." When you're vulnerable, you acknowledge weakness, you acknowledge even failure.

I've learned that our kids have learned much more from our mistakes than they have learned from our successes. So in our times as a family together, we would often share where we'd made mistakes along the way. This helps people. It helps the congregation to know when a pastor has made a mistake and comes back later to apologize or to acknowledge the mistake made. He loses nothing and gains everything. They appreciate the honesty of acknowledging a wrong or a mistake—most likely an honest mistake.

One of the ways to live a healthy, happier life is to not drag anchors. Anchors are things that were done wrong but never made right. Statements that were erroneous that we need to clarify to individuals. How wise we are when we set the record straight.

Paul ended his list by pointing his finger and saying, "Stay away from people like that!" (2 Timothy 3:5). Avoid them. Don't make friends with them. If you're not careful, you'll adopt their habits.

When I was a teenager and ran around with a couple of tough kids, my mother would say to me, "Every time you're with Eugene and Freddy, you get in trouble." I denied it because I thought I was one of the smartest guys on the planet. Eventually, I realized Freddy and Eugene were not good for me. The more I hung around them, the more I got into trouble. I learned the hard way to stay away from people like that.

Stand Firm on Scripture

Yes, we live in savage times, and we must watch out for people who cause trouble. The evil of these last days can get a foothold in our lives because evil is deceptive. It isn't up front. It doesn't come across as brazenly wrong, but it is wrong. Remember, Lucifer "disguises himself as an angel of light" (2 Corinthians 11:14). He loves for you to think of him as this little, red-skinned creature with a pitchfork and a tail. Ridiculous.

I have a little tiny statue of the devil in my library. People who visit my study see it and wonder what I am doing with a devil figure. When you press the top, a little pushup comes out that says, "Go to hell." At least it used to say that. I painted over it! Now, it says, "Surprise!"

The devil will surprise you. He's the most attractive creature that's ever been created. He's the most appealing creature. He's the most persuasive creature, and he can make people deaf to truth or blind to reality because he loves deception.

You know how you break through deception? Never forget this. *Discernment.*

The simplest definition of discernment is "knowing right from wrong," which we must teach little children because they don't have discernment. We must teach them not to trust every adult who offers them a ride home from school. That's why parents warn them not to take money or gifts from people, who often have wrong intentions. Children are innocent. They aren't aware of evil in the world.

There are Christians who are equally gullible. They don't realize that something that looks good may not be good. Something that sounds right may not be right. If you're gullible, you'll buy it. You'll support it. In reality, if you had the discernment to probe deeply, to see behind the mask, you would discover it is as evil as it can be. How else does a serial killer get by with what he does, or a rapist? How else does a child molester carry on his godless, terrible lifestyle? *Deception*.

Don't think that because a man wears a robe and looks charming or handsome or stands at a very ornate pulpit that he's trustworthy. Listen to him carefully. Listen to what he's not saying. Pay attention to what he addresses and how he says it, how he refers to himself, how he deals with others when there aren't many around. Pay attention to his private life.

Now, here was Timothy in Ephesus, surrounded by false teachers in the church. Paul had warned the Ephesian elders that "false teachers, like vicious wolves, will come in among you," and they "will rise up and distort the truth in order to draw a following" (Acts 20:29–30).

It wasn't long before they forgot Paul's words, however, and little by little, the church at Ephesus began to drift. In Revelation, the Lord rebuked the church, saying, "You have left your first love" (Revelation 2:4 NASB). This church that began so strong ultimately weakened and drifted.

My warning to all of us is this: *beware.* Troublemakers with evil motives love to prey on the sheep.

So how do we stand firm in these difficult times?

Timothy could go all the way back to his childhood and remember that he was taught the Holy Scriptures. But now Paul was telling Timothy to dig deeper. To turn his knowledge into conviction. Timothy must make sure to stand firm in his beliefs.

The same is true for all of us. You'll be one who will have to stand up on your own and say, "I cannot go along with the majority opinion. Here's the reason why." And then, state the Scripture that gives you the basis of your decision. *Your discernment based on Scripture will help you stand firm.*

Paul reminded us of the central role of the Scriptures in our faith:

> *All Scripture is inspired by God and is useful to teach us what is true and to make us realize what is wrong in our lives. It corrects us when we are wrong and teaches us to do what is right. God uses it to prepare and equip his people to do every good work.*
> (2 Timothy 3:16–17)

Three doctrinal terms help to explain the Scripture's role: *revelation*, *inspiration*, and *illumination*. Revelation is God giving us His Word, and that act of God is complete. Inspiration refers to the recording of His Word supernaturally so that it has now been preserved for us in a reliable way that we can read it. The Greek term for *inspiration* literally means, "God-breathed." So when you see words in the Bible, you're seeing the breath of God in word form, in verbal form. "All Scripture is God-breathed."

Revelation is over. Inspiration has finished. We have the Scriptures in the 66 books of our Bible. But illumination continues today. Illumination is understanding what you have heard and read in the Scriptures.

The Bible is like no other literature you'll ever read. This is God-breathed literature. That's why you need your own place to study it for it to become profitable to you. Don't just read it on the fly. There may be moments when that's all the time you have, but make sure you have a place to study it. Have a pen, have a pad, have a journal. Write things down that you are observing. Pass them on to those in your group, those in your family, those you love.

God's Word is a priceless treasure. It's beneficial for:

- Teaching "us what is true"—that's doctrine
- Making "us realize what is wrong in our lives"—that's reproof
- Telling "us when we're wrong"—that's correction
- Helping "us to do what is right"—that's training

No other book on earth will do that for you like the Bible. That's why I've opened the Book for all my years in the pulpit, read from it, and taught from it.

Now, what if we just ignore all this? What if we just let troublemakers have their way and don't stand firm on the Scriptures? The following story gives an example of how that could happen and how to fix it.

What It Takes to Stand Firm

I received a phone call from a pastor who was brokenhearted. His voice shook as he spoke, "Chuck, I'm at a church that's gone through the two previous pastors rather quickly, and before those two, another man left quicker than many people thought he would. Now, I'm the pastor. The reason they left was because of a man in our church whose goal is to drive pastors out! He's a bully. We're losing our young people. They don't want to be around bullies. They resent him. We're getting ready to lose our youth worker. What in the world do I do?"

I challenged him: "Do you really want to deal with this?"

He said, "I think I do. But the way you say that makes me wonder if I want to hear your answer!"

I said, "You can't allow the troublemaker to continue. Do you have trustworthy elders?"

"Yes, I do," he replied.

"Do they stand for the truth?"

The pastor replied, "I think they do."

I answered: "Then bring this man before the elders. Confront him. Remember, the two things troublemakers don't want are exposure and confrontation. I would imagine the previous pastors sort of tucked their tails between their legs and just left without many words."

He said, "I have a feeling that's what happened. Maybe that's why they were so desperate for me to come as the new pastor. And, by the way, the man has said to his friends that he plans to run me off. So, I'm next."

I said, "No, you're not. Bring him in and tell him he's a bully. He has run off the previous pastors, and he's not running off this one. Make sure your elders say more than you do, by the way. Let them speak for you. Make sure they're on your side. And then remove the man from the church."

A long pause followed. Then he said, "Remove the man from the church."

I said, "Yes, get him out!"

"Can I quote you?" he asked.

I said, "Yes, quote me! Then call me back and tell me what happened."

A few weeks passed, and my phone rang. It was my friend. He said, "Hey, Chuck, he's gone! It was a great moment to see him walk out. I don't think we'll ever see him again."

I said, "Great, unless he changes his heart, then he's welcome back. Who knows, he may get saved!"

My friend replied, "You want to know something else interesting? We've already begun to get our youth back. It's a whole new chapter for our church."

I said to him, "I'm proud of you. You know what you've done? You've protected the flock."

That's what good shepherds do. We don't just preach. We don't just pray. We don't just read Scripture. When we're not in private meetings, we are doing the hard work of shepherding. Elders do that, and hopefully some of you who are teachers do that. It's the thing I enjoy the least about ministry, but it's important.

Paul listed nineteen characteristics of troublemakers to watch out for. Now, not every one of these calls for removal, but some of them do. Don't be afraid of that. Stand your ground.

Remember what Jesus said to Judas? Judas was there for the Last Supper, and Jesus said to him, "Whatever you do, do quickly." In other words, get out. He went out and John says in his gospel, "And it was night." I've always been intrigued by that detail. The darkness surrounded Judas and went all the way into his heart. He was a son of perdition. You know how deceitful he was? The disciples had no idea why he went out. They still trusted him. Something about Judas was so deceptive. Only Jesus discerned the truth.

Beware. Look around. Pay attention. Teach your children to be discerning, and let's teach one another to keep walking in the right so wrong will never have its way in Christ's church.

Thank You, Father, for telling us the truth. Thank You for confronting us when sin needs to be pointed out. For leading us to repentance that we might trust in You with all our hearts and not in ourselves. Deliver us from troublemakers like we've read about today. Give us strength to live above the drag of this old sin nature. Make us aware of the power of deception. And keep us strong by Your grace for years to come, should Christ tarry. In the name of Jesus, I pray these things. Amen.

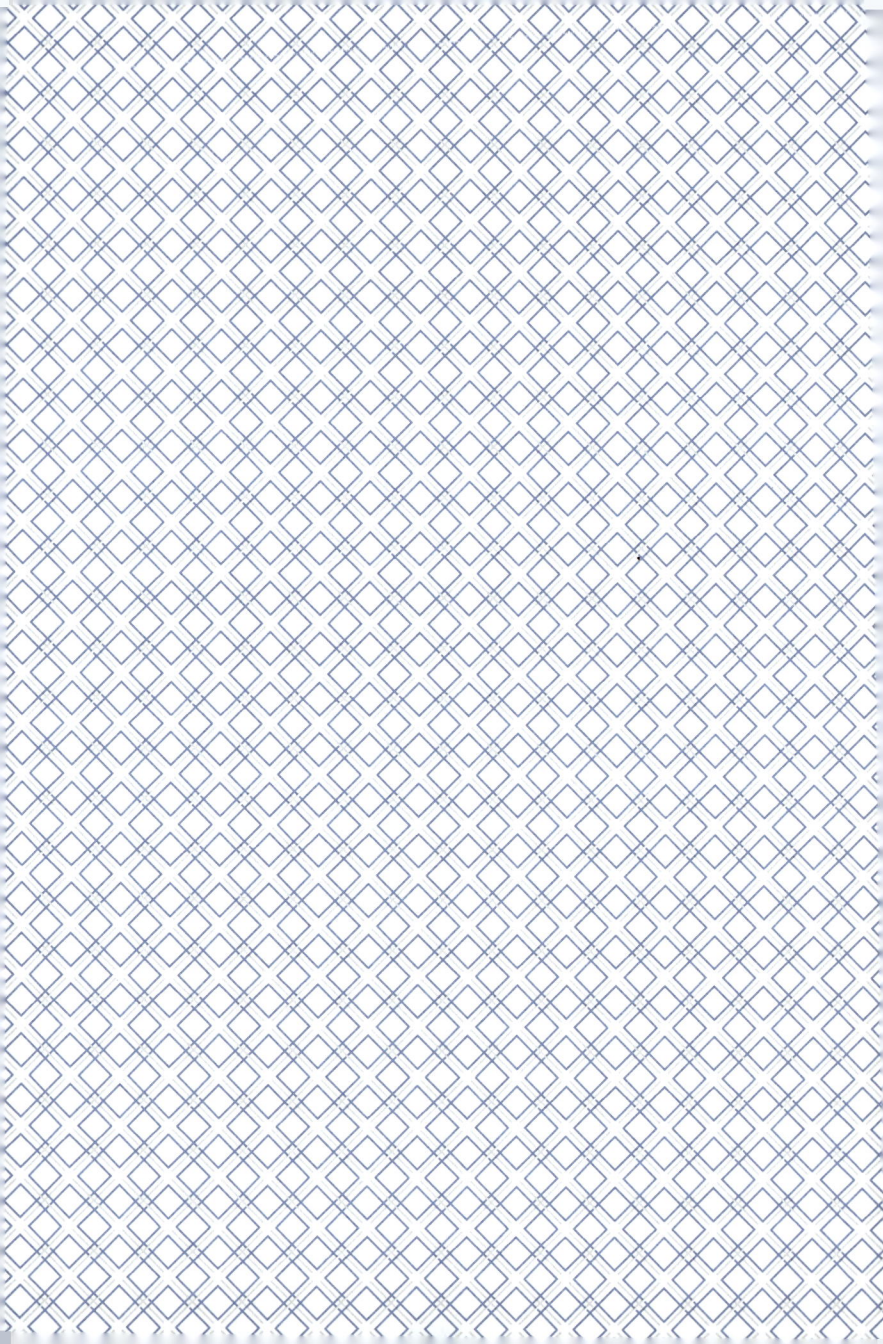

CHAPTER 4

Look Up
Are You Using Your Gifts?

Delivered October 13, 2024

*I solemnly urge you in the presence of God and
Christ Jesus, who will someday judge the living
and the dead when he comes to set up his Kingdom:
Preach the word of God. . . . Work at telling others
the Good News, and fully carry out the ministry
God has given you.*

2 TIMOTHY 4:1–2, 5

Do not enter the ministry if you can help it." Now who
on earth would have the audacity to make a statement
like that?

Maybe it was some jaded former pastor who was
burnt out, had given up, and was now throwing rocks at
the church. Or maybe it was an out-and-out atheist who,
at every chance he could get, took shots at the church
and those who lead the church.

In fact, those are the words of Charles Haddon Spurgeon—the prince of the pulpit in England during the Victorian era! He was anything but jaded about ministry and certainly not an atheist!

He took his first church when he was 17 years old, and before he turned 20, the New Park Street Chapel, a Baptist church, asked him to become their pastor. Spurgeon accepted that call and spent the rest of his life as their pastor until he died at the young age of 57.

The church grew immediately. When the old chapel filled up, they built an addition and then another addition but even that couldn't hold the crowds. So, they erected the Metropolitan Tabernacle which could house 6,000 people, but that was soon packed out.

People would stand in the snow waiting for the doors to open so they might be able to find a seat to hear the preacher. Over the course of his ministry, the church had added over 14,000 members, which was unheard of in England.

Spurgeon's remarkable gift spread beyond England. He became known worldwide. After his death, those who loved his ministry printed and distributed one sermon every week for 25 years. They had to cease operations due to lack of funds and paper shortages during World War I—not because they ran out of material! I call that prolific.

Spurgeon penned the words, "Do not enter the ministry if you can help it," in his fine book, *Lectures to My Students*, dated 1875. Why in the world would this man write words like that?

He knew the cost of leadership. He knew the sacrifices of fame. He knew what it was to have ugly false rumors spread about him. He endured constant criticism from those who envied him, especially from fellow preachers whose congregations were not his size. There probably is no career filled with more envying people than the ministry. It's all about size. It's all about me. It's all about what I've done. It's all about how many people come.

Spurgeon knew none of those envious feelings. Fame depressed him. In fact, he said on one occasion that he wished he could escape to the United States just to get out of the eye of the critic. Impossible! Escape from criticism never happens for those in ministry.

Wherever Spurgeon went, he was news. Whatever he said and whatever he did was scrutinized and analyzed by those who were not qualified to do it. He became weary of that. There's a chapter in the book, *Lectures to My Students*, where he addressed his own depression. I admire such vulnerability.

People throw rocks at those in the ministry and say ugly things about them and pass rumors that aren't true. If they don't pick on the minister, they will pick on his wife. If not on his wife, they'll pick on his kids.

Some of my kids told me while they were growing up, there were teachers who said, "You don't know the answer to the test and you're Chuck Swindoll's daughter or son?" How insulting. How unfair. Does having a father as a preacher make you suddenly know all the answers? No, it doesn't.

So don't enter the ministry if you can help it. Or as Harry Truman put it, "If you can't stand the heat, get out of the kitchen."

If God calls you into the ministry, however, He will give you the grace to persevere—just as He gave grace to Paul to persevere through his hardships. Paul's critics threw actual stones at him!

The gems of wisdom Paul passed to Timothy and to all those in ministry were mined from the severest of circumstances. His counsel in his Second Letter to Timothy included a solemn charge followed by five commands. Even if you haven't been called into pastoral ministry, Paul's words will encourage you to persevere in whatever ways you serve the Lord as you use your gift for Him.

A Solemn Charge to Use Your Gift

Paul charged Timothy to use his gift like an older pastor commissioning a younger pastor at an ordination service.

> *I solemnly urge you in the presence of*
> *God and Christ Jesus, who will someday*
> *judge the living and the dead when he*
> *comes to set up his Kingdom.*
> (2 Timothy 4:1)

Paul was telling his son in the faith, "Timothy, your calling comes from heaven. You're not a hired gun for some church or some board. You are a minister of Christ called by God to fulfill your position. Hirelings are hired. Dedicated ministers are called."

Callings come in different shapes and sizes. Mine is different from yours, his is different from hers, hers is different from his. But the calling is there, and you'll notice it's called *solemn* because it comes straight from heaven. Talk about a high calling!

Timothy, who tended to be timid, ministered in the fast-moving pagan city of Ephesus. False teachers surrounded the church like wolves ready to attack the flock. "Timothy, listen to me," Paul said with urgency. "Remember first of all that your calling comes from the living God."

God calls us to the church, but we serve the Savior and Lord Jesus Christ. He is the God-man, undiminished deity and true humanity, unmixed in one person forever. He's the head of the church. It belongs to Him, and, as the One who leads the church, He alone has "absolute authority to judge" (John 5:22). We stand before Him.

When Jesus returns to set up His kingdom, He will look at our outer life and inner life. He will expose the secrets. He will reveal the whole truth. Nothing will be hidden from Him.

We should take our call seriously because Christ's judgment is greater for ministers than for others, and the reason is because so much is at stake. Ministers influence people's souls, and they can lead them astray with erroneous teaching. That's why James gave the following warning, which sounds like Spurgeon's warning:

> *Dear brothers and sisters, not many of you*
> *should become teachers in the church, for*
> *we who teach will be judged more strictly.*
> (James 3:1)

The standard I face is higher than the one you face because I'm in ministry. That doesn't mean I'm better than you; it means I'm going to be judged "more strictly" than you will be. Don't think that doesn't haunt me at times.

I answer to a judge who is fair and omniscient. That's good enough for me. He knows the truth. Things you don't even think about regarding me, He knows it's all. It's in clear view to Him.

In a courtroom, we take an oath: "I swear to tell the whole truth and nothing but the truth, so help me God." When you say that in the courtroom, it should put a little chill up your spine. That's just a courtroom of people before a human judge. But when we stand before the divine Judge, He knows the truth about our lives before we even raise our right hand.

Paul's charge is solemn and all-consuming. What does it consist of, specifically? Paul explains the minister's duties next.

Five Commands to Follow

Paul instructed Timothy to fulfill his calling by following five commands. You can draw principles from these commands to apply in whatever role you may fill as you serve the Lord. Here is Paul's list for Timothy:

> *Preach the word of God. Be prepared,*
> *whether the time is favorable or not.*
> *Patiently correct, rebuke, and encourage*
> *your people with good teaching.*
> (2 Timothy 4:2)

First, *preach*. The Greek word is *kerux*, and it refers to a herald. Heralds stood before the king, received his message, and declared it with a loud voice in the public square. They didn't change the message to make it easier to accept. They announced the king's words without altering one of them, conveying the king's message just as they received it.

Likewise, we take our King's message and declare it without shaping or twisting it with our opinions. Our opinions are worth nothing more than anyone else's opinions. Opinions aren't inspired. People don't bank their lives on opinions. So, we study the Book and herald a message people can count on. We preach the Word of God.

Second, *be prepared*. We must be prepared to declare God's message all the time, whether it's early or late, whether it's hot or cold, whether we feel like it or we don't feel like it, whether the crowd is large or small.

I remember our first place of service after seminary at Grace Bible Church. Every Sunday, the church was packed with people who would come from all over to hear Dr. Pentecost preach. I was an unknown assistant with a name people mispronounced, "Swindle."

On Sundays when he was absent, guess who would preach? That's right. *Me!* A leader in the church said to me one day, "Chuck, just remember, your popularity here is a borrowed popularity." He was right. He wasn't criticizing me. He was giving me a wake-up call to the reality of ministry. His point was this: "Don't think you're going to pack it out wherever you go."

When I left Grace Bible Church and took my first senior pastor role in New England, I thought I would get New England straightened out in about six months. I didn't even learn my way around in six months! Our congregation never grew large. One Fourth of July Sunday there were seven people in the pews, and three were Swindolls.

When we focus on proclaiming the Word, we stop counting the number of people. We don't brag about how big our church is or criticize those whose church isn't as big as ours. And we don't feel bad because ours isn't growing. God determines the size. It's not our job to fill it up. It's our job to preach the Word of God.

I've done that for more than 60 years in the ministry, and I tell you it works. Be prepared, whether it's comfortable or uncomfortable, whether they're loving you or criticizing you. Preach the Word of God. Stay at it "in season, out of season," as the King James Version puts it. When you're well or when you're not well. When others go to their lake houses for the weekend and you're there preaching, *stay at it!* Do it in season and out of season.

When I was discharged from the Marine Corps, I said to Cynthia, "You know what, honey? While I was overseas, I volunteered with The Navigators, and I realized that I'm called to the ministry." She was thrilled!

Before joining the Marines, I had been training to be a machinist. For four-and-a-half years, I went to night school and learned math and mechanical engineering related to machinery. Then, when I had to fulfill a military obligation, I chose the Marine Corps.

In the Marines, I learned discipline. I learned how a platoon of 70 men could be transformed into a fighting team, and I learned to lead that group. I learned to throw hand grenades. I learned to make amphibious landings. I also learned a lot about depravity because I lived in a barracks, and I heard profanity I had never heard before.

Depravity, when it's raw, is filthy. Ninety percent of the men in our barracks had a venereal disease. Prostitutes were brought in by the United States government to service the Marines like they were animals. I came through all that by the grace of God without failing in my faithfulness to my wife.

When I changed my career path from machinist to minister, I needed to get properly trained, so I decided to go to Dallas Theological Seminary . . . however, I didn't meet the requirements for entering graduate school. I wound up in the office of Dr. Campbell, the registrar, who would determine whether to accept me as a student. I was fresh out of the Marines with my flat-top haircut sitting beside Cynthia, who was dressed in a beautiful white outfit. I told him, "I'm really not qualified for this." He said, "I know." And he was right.

He said, "I'll give you a few tests, and I want you to fill in the answers with as many Scriptures as you can." I took those tests, and he contacted Cynthia and me two weeks later.

"You know what, Chuck," Dr. Campbell said. "We're going to take a risk. We're going to accept you on probation." I thought, *Praise the God of heaven, grace is coming my way*.

In the interview, he asked me a crucial question: "Would you be happy doing anything but ministry for the rest of your life?" I had never thought of that question before. I looked at my darling wife and I blinked and she blinked, and I looked back at Dr. Campbell. I said, "No, sir, I would not be happy or fulfilled in anything but ministry. If I can't get training here, I'm going to get it somewhere, and I give you my word, I'll do it for the rest of my life as long as I have breath in my lungs." Later, he said to me that if I had any other answer, he would not have accepted me.

I loved all four years at DTS. *I was made for this*, I thought. I went in as a student on probation, so I assumed I'd be sitting on the back row, treated like a third-class citizen. Never. Not one professor ever referred to me as a probationary student. Not one student even knew that I was on probation. Only the registrar.

Because I was a probationary student, pride was never a problem for me. I sat among other students who were very bright. They had rings on their fingers from prestigious universities. I'd never been in one. I didn't envy them; I admired them. Some were working on a second master's degree to go on and get a doctorate.

How privileged I was to be asked while at seminary by Dr. Pentecost to be an assistant at Grace Bible Church. I loved it! When I pastored in New England, it was a whole new set of circumstances. I moved from there to pastor a church in Irving, Texas, and it was another set of circumstances. Then, on to Fullerton, California, and it was another set of circumstances.

Later, I became the president of my alma mater, Dallas Theological Seminary, and it was a brand-new set of circumstances. *A probationary student became seminary president!* I think most of the students didn't know that, but they should have because if I could make it through DTS, anybody could.

If you think you're not good enough to be in ministry, forget that nonsense. You don't have to be good enough. You just need to *trust* enough. Lean on God with all your heart.

Being prepared to preach the Word of God is all about character. Maybe there was something about doing amphibious landings or training troops for combat or throwing grenades or wearing gas masks or running through obstacle courses or living in barracks and learning about depravity that prepared me for ministry.

Nothing to this day shocks me that a sinner can tell me. Pimps in Los Angeles have come into my office wanting to talk to me about Jesus. Never once was I shocked. I've had the offscouring of the world talk to me about their lives. I'm never shocked. Of course not. They don't have Christ. They can't possibly live a clean life. I never expected my fellow Marines to live a pure life until they knew Jesus.

J. Vernon McGee's statement says it well: "God didn't call us on this earth to clean up the fishbowl, he called us to fish." So don't try to clean people up before they come to Christ. He takes us just like we are—depraved, rotten, sorry, sinful people. He gives us two legs to stand on and a heart for Him. And then He begins to build us into Christ-like people—which leads us to Paul's next command.

Third, *patiently correct*. Correcting people means that we call sin, sin. I've never seen anyone change his or her life of sin to a life of righteousness who did not first realize he or she was doing wrong. People must acknowledge their depravity and admit, *I have a miserable lifestyle*. Only then do they want to live a kingdom life. To want God to change their hearts. To clean up their mouths. To free their minds from lust and greed. To help them stop being selfish or conceited or arrogant. Patiently correcting people points them God's way.

Fourth, *rebuke*. The next command is to rebuke, which simply means to help people understand the consequences of sin. If people don't turn to Christ, they will suffer judgment—which doesn't include purgatory. There is no such place. We don't get a second chance.

No one can earn his or her way into heaven. We get into heaven only through faith in Christ by the grace of God. God packaged the gift of salvation in Christ and places the gift before us and says, "Take it or leave it." I can't make people take it, but it is my job to offer it.

I used to worry about people's responses to God's Word. I used to think, *Maybe I'm responsible for their response.* Are you kidding? I'm responsible to apply God's Word for myself. I can't do that for anyone else. My job is to deliver God's gift and get out of the way. I sleep better, I eat better, I relax better, and I worry less.

Fifth, *encourage*. I'm so glad Paul ended his commands with the word, *encourage*. People need hope. They need to know that there's life beyond their sinfulness, that they don't have to always be an ill-tempered person or live negatively. They can choose Christ's joy. They can take responsibility rather than blame others. They can forgive instead of holding a grudge and trust God rather than worry.

I'm not the reason people come to church. The Spirit of God is at work, using His Word, drawing people like a magnet to a place where truth is told, and that's the way, hopefully, it will always be.

The Urgent Need to Use Your Gift ═══════

Using our gifts to proclaim God's Word is crucial in our day because so many ministers have drifted away from this essential core of their calling. Paul forewarned that these times would come:

> *For a time is coming when people will
> no longer listen to sound and wholesome
> teaching. They will follow their own desires
> and will look for teachers who will tell them
> whatever their itching ears want to hear.
> They will reject the truth and chase after
> myths.* (2 Timothy 4:3–4)

People have "itching ears." Have your ears ever itched? I wear hearing aids, so my ears itch sometimes and I just have to scratch them. Oh, man, there are few things better than scratching that itch! I tell Cynthia, "Don't talk right now, honey. I'm scratching my itchy ear!"

Well, Paul was saying that these people want sermons that scratch them where they're itching. They want ministers to tell them how great they are. They don't want to hear about the consequences of sin or the need for repentance. They don't want to know about that messy stuff. So, some ministers set aside the Scriptures and tell people what they want to hear so they will come back.

I care more about telling the truth than whether people come back. And if they come back, they must want more of the truth because that's all they're going to hear from me.

I heard an interview between a very keen interviewer and a well-known televangelist. No need to mention his name, but he was well-published, well-known. The interviewer asked, "Now, we haven't talked about sin. Do you . . ." and before he could finish the sentence, the preacher said, "No, no, I never use that word, *sin*. People don't want to hear about sin."

Do you know what this preacher preaches? *Myths.* I know, that sounds strange, but that's the word Paul used—"they will reject the truth and chase after myths." Hearing stories makes people feel good. It scratches their itch.

Paul was urgent about his charge to Timothy because he knew that he would not be around much longer. It was up to Timothy to preach the Word after Paul was gone. So Paul prodded the young pastor to get at it! He was saying, "Say it right. Do it well. Stop being timid. False teachers aren't timid! They'll walk all over you. You need to have guts, Timothy."

I learned to have guts in the Marine Corps. I learned to stand alone, to run past temptation, and get to the Bible study. If you run, you can't lust. It works! Try it. When you linger, you're finished, so don't do that. "Run from anything that stimulates youthful lusts. Instead pursue righteous living," Paul wrote (2 Timothy 2:22). If you run, you'll sweat and it hurts, but it doesn't matter. You'll stay pure.

What would help Timothy avoid these pitfalls in using his gifts? What will help us? Paul tells us:

> *But you should keep a clear mind in every situation. Don't be afraid of suffering for the Lord. Work at telling others the Good News, and fully carry out the ministry God has given you.* (4:5)

With a clear mind, we must stay focused on what's most important, so we won't get caught up in the comparative stuff. We won't get competitive or worry about what people say. We'll be willing to tell others about Christ, even if it means we suffer.

You should have heard the names the other soldiers called me in the Marine Corps. I was called Friar, the Reverend. I didn't care. I cared about people's souls going to heaven. In our Quonset hut of a few dozen guys, before I left, I'd led seven men to Christ. In the Marine Corps that's a revival!

I paid a price living in the barracks as a Christian. It's the same for Christian young people living in a college dorm where sexual sin is rampant. We must teach our young people not to look at pornography. The first step toward ruining your family is pornography. You may think that nobody knows because your door is closed and your blinds are closed and you're all alone. But you're ruining your life. You say, "Well, I'm addicted, Chuck." I have a gift for you, Jesus Christ. He'll break your addictions. It won't be easy and it won't be quick, but Jesus has never met an obstacle He couldn't clear. He'll help you do that.

Paul told Timothy to "work at telling others the Good News." Paul was passionate in his appeal. "Never stop, Timothy," Paul was saying. "For the rest of your life, do it. When they cut my head off, Timothy, do it. When I'm gone, when you're out there on your own, do it!"

I admire the men who have modeled that for me. I was trained by them in seminary. When I graduated, I didn't have a clue where I'd be going, and then God stepped in. I just focused on the cross where He died for me and saved me by His grace. I set my sights toward the cross, and I always will. I married a woman who did the same thing. We've got a family that does the same thing. Are we perfect? Far from it. Give up perfection. That's Jesus' realm. We're only human, but we're sincere, and we're real.

The winds of culture are strong, and the current of compromise is fast these days. We can fall into all kinds of gimmicks, fads, movements, and myths. We don't need another movement or another myth. We just need to preach the Word of God, and that's enough.

> *Thank You, Lord, for showing me the truth and then helping me realize that I had nothing to do with creating it. My job is to proclaim it, and it's the same for all who are in this work. Thank You for Paul who modeled it so well when he finally was blinded on the road to Damascus and Your Son turned his life around. Thank You for our mentors who give us hope and encouragement that we can make it by Your grace, and only by Your grace. In Christ's name we pray, amen.*

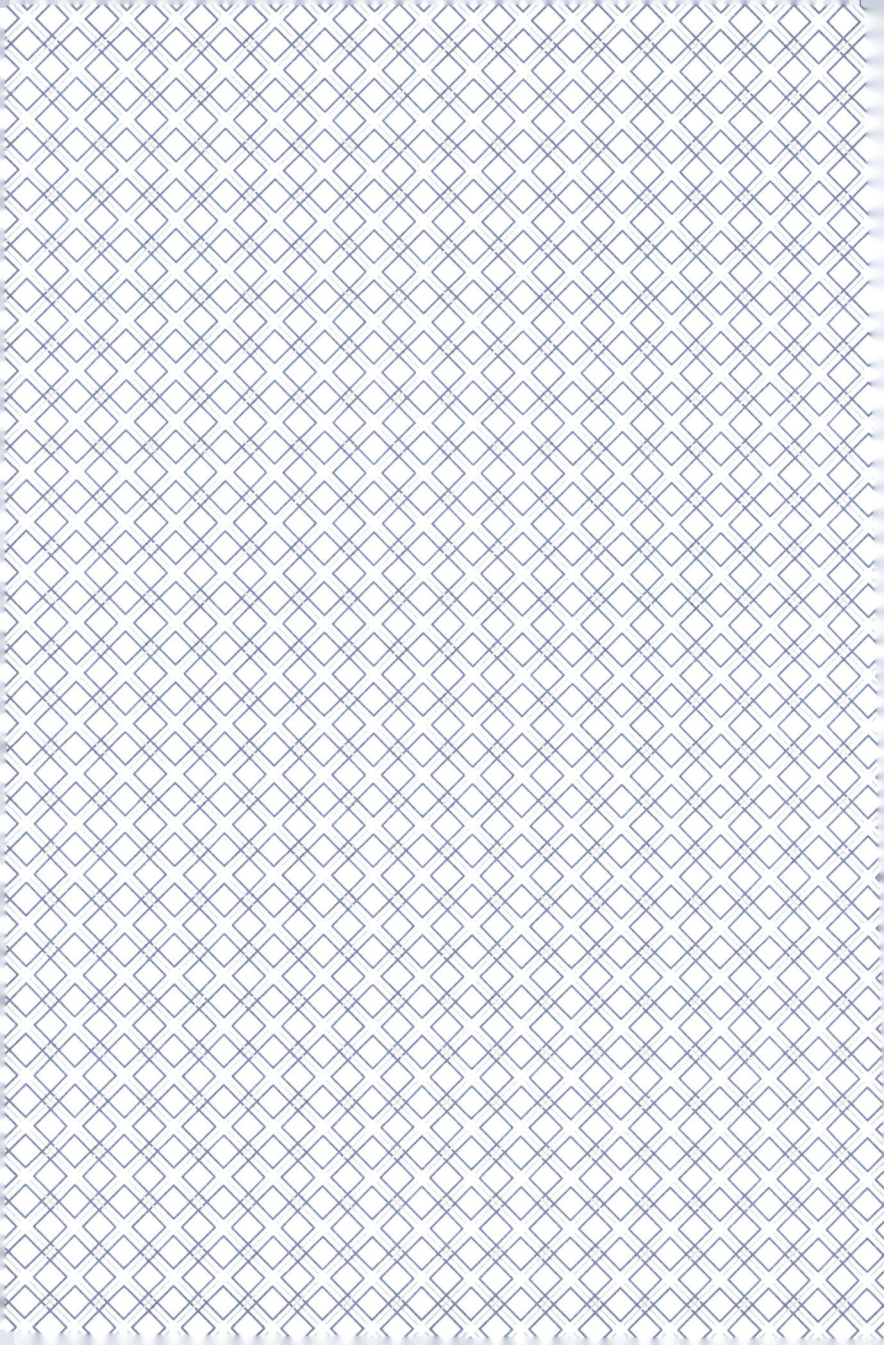

CHAPTER 5

Look Beyond

Will You Focus on Eternity?

Delivered October 20, 2024
(Two Days after Chuck's 90th Birthday)

As for me, my life has already been poured out as an offering to God. The time of my death is near. I have fought the good fight, I have finished the race, and I have remained faithful. And now the prize awaits me—the crown of righteousness, which the Lord, the righteous Judge, will give me on the day of his return. And the prize is not just for me but for all who eagerly look forward to his appearing.

2 TIMOTHY 4:6–8

Nero must have gloated over his most recent achievement. Finally, after persecuting and torturing and killing thousands who called Jesus their Lord, he was able to say to the Senate, "Their major spokesman has been captured and declared guilty. I've had him flogged and placed in the Mamertine Prison, awaiting execution."

Nero, that demented ruler of the Roman Empire, slept on silk sheets and lived surrounded by garish decorations in his opulent palace. He took sadistic delight in the cruelest forms of punishment, having Christians torn apart by wild animals. Now he had Paul just where he wanted him, finally silenced.

Well, not really. Paul had one more letter to write. Sitting in a foul-smelling and rat-infested dungeon cell, Paul, as his final act of ministry, wrote to a man with most of his ministry life ahead of him—Timothy, with whom Paul traveled for years. Now he had the opportunity to write Timothy one last letter.

Paul was not concerned about the filth of the dungeon nor the pain he suffered, which only worsened with each day. Not once in 2 Timothy did Paul come near complaining about his circumstances or the stench of that cell. The eyes of his heart looked toward the future.

He was thinking of Timothy, over 800 miles east in Ephesus. Paul, in this dungeon under the streets of Rome, knew what was ahead for him. One of these days, he would hear boots of the death squad marching toward him above that grate. They would pull him from the dungeon and march him out of the city in chains. The lictor would bend him over the stump, raise the long-handled axe, sharpened to a razor's edge, and bring it down on the back of Paul's neck, sending his head rolling into the dust. Paul knew what was ahead of him.

What was in Paul's mind as he awaited his execution? He longed for Timothy's company during this final hour. "Come before winter," Paul asked with a yearning heart (2 Timothy 4:21 NASB). I'd like to believe that Timothy came before winter and brought with him the cloak Paul had left at Troas, along with some books Paul requested, the scriptural scrolls that were Paul's personal Bible. Also traveling with Timothy would be John Mark, whom Paul had once written off, but later realized that he was profitable to him for the ministry. "Bring Mark with you when you come," Paul wrote (4:11). I want to believe they made it to the cell and were allowed entrance for a brief visit as the men embraced.

I wonder what they prayed. I wonder which song or hymn they sang. I wonder what Paul and Timothy said to one another as they thought back over those years of travel together.

As you read your Bible, allow your imagination to float along with you. Relive the scenes you uncover. Otherwise, these words appear on the page and you simply turn to the next page. Pause. Take time to let the wonder in.

If Paul were in prison today, I imagine him breaking into the hymn, "Praise the Savior, Ye Who Know Him."

Praise the Savior, ye who know Him!
Who can tell how much we owe Him?
Gladly let us render to Him
All we are and have.

Jesus is the name that charms us,
He for conflict fits and arms us;
Nothing moves and nothing harms us
While we trust in Him.

Trust in Him, you saints, forever;
He is faithful, changing never;
Neither force nor guile can sever
Those He loves from Him.

Keep us, Lord, O keep us cleaving
To Thyself and still believing,
Till the hour of our receiving
Promised joys with Thee.

Then we shall be where we would be,
Then we shall be what we should be;
Things that are not now, nor could be,
Soon shall be our own.[1]

What a reassuring hymn to sing in desperate circumstances. Or, perhaps Paul would sing, "Majestic Sweetness Sits Enthroned."

> Majestic sweetness sits enthroned
> Upon the Savior's brow;
> His head with radiant glories crowned,
> His lips with grace o'erflow,
> His lips with grace o'erflow.
>
> He saw me plunged in deep despair,
> And flew to my relief;
> For me He bore the shameful cross,
> And carries all my grief,
> And carries all my grief.[2]

What song would you sing in a prison cell if you were someday incarcerated for your faith? What Scripture would you quote to another that you have committed to memory, knowing that you'll not be allowed to have a copy of the Bible with you?

When Paul wrote to his beloved son in the faith, Timothy, he was living out his final days. It was Paul's desire to warn Timothy, to encourage him, to stir up the gift within him, and to prompt him to step up. He was bracing Timothy for storms on the horizon: "Don't be afraid of suffering; savage times are coming."

If you had lived in that era of extreme persecution, you might wonder if wrong was winning and right was lost. James Russell Lowell's words voice the feelings of the persecuted through the centuries, as well as their enduring faith:

> Truth, forever on the scaffold,
>   Wrong forever on the throne,—
> Yet that scaffold sways the future,
>   and, behind the dim unknown,
> Standeth God within the shadow,
>   keeping watch above his own.[3]

Nero thought he had all the power, but, on His celestial throne, God was keeping watch and keeping score. In the end, Paul wore the victor's crown, while Nero's crown was tossed in the trash heap. There's a beautiful irony when you contrast Paul with Nero. One man put it well. He said, "Today, people name their sons Paul and their dogs Nero." God will balance the scales in the end.

Never forget the words of the prophet Nahum about God's justice and sovereign rule:

> *The LORD is slow to anger and great in*
>   *power,*
> *And will not at all acquit the wicked.*
> *The LORD has His way*
> *In the whirlwind and in the storm,*
> *And the clouds are the dust of His feet.*
> (Nahum 1:3 NKJV)

Finish the Race

Paul wrote not as a depressed man but as an urgent man. He told Timothy, "I am already being poured out as a drink offering" (2 Timothy 4:6 NASB). Strange words to us but not to those in Paul's day. Ancient Jews would use those words to describe what they would do when they would pour out red wine at the base of an altar. The wine represented the blood of the sacrificial lamb poured out in death. Similarly, Paul's life was draining out of him like blood on an altar. Paul said, "The time of my departure has come" (4:6). There was no fear in Paul's heart, however, nor reluctance about the reality of his situation.

What a beautiful word, *departure*. Three images emerge from the Greek word, translated "departure." One is of an oxen that is suddenly unyoked from its burden, whether it's pulling a cart or carrying a load. He's unyoked from the burden.

The word also refers to pulling up tent pegs, striking a tent, and moving on to another location. It's also used to describe loosening ropes at a pier so a large ship can move out into the deep and begin its voyage.

All three metaphors apply to Paul's life. He was saying, "The time of my being unburdened is upon me. I am unyoking from the cares of this age. My tent pegs are pulling up, and I'm moving on."

Maybe Paul recalled and reaffirmed what he had written in previous letters:

> *For to me, to live is Christ, and to die is gain.*
> (Philippians 1:21 NASB)

> *"Where, O Death, is your victory? Where, O Death, is your sting?" The sting of death is sin, and the power of sin is the Law; but thanks be to God, who gives us the victory through our Lord Jesus Christ.*
> (1 Corinthians 15:55–57 NASB)

> *I am convinced that neither death, nor life,*
> *nor angels, nor principalities, nor things*
> *present, nor things to come, nor powers,*
> *nor height, nor depth, nor any other created*
> *thing will be able to separate us from the*
> *love of God that is in Christ Jesus our Lord.*
> (Romans 8:38–39 NASB)

Paul was confident that though the Romans could separate his head from his body, they could never separate him from the love of his Lord. His destiny was *secure* in Christ.

Interestingly, Paul addressed his present situation first. "My life is poured out as a drink offering." That's now. "The time of my departure has come." That's now. Then he looked to the past.

> *I have fought the good fight, I have finished*
> *the race, and I have remained faithful.*
> (2 Timothy 4:7)

I like the way Paul put it: "I have fought the *good* fight." It wasn't a needless fight. It wasn't a selfish fight. It wasn't a silly skirmish, arguing over some detail that doesn't matter. No, his was a fight for the truth. A fight against false teaching. A fight against those who would hurt the believers, who would take advantage of God's people, who would put obstacles in the way of those who carry the message of Christ. He was saying, "I've stood in the defense of many. The fight I have fought was a good fight."

Paul put the verb at the end of the sentence to emphasize it—"The race, I have finished." He didn't just run the race, but he finished it. His life was almost over. We read that statement and bite our lip to keep from weeping . . . but not Paul. He wasn't sad. God set the course, and Paul believed the Lord led him all the way from the road to Damascus where he was converted to the prison where he was now held. God led him all the way, and he had run that race through the tape across the finish line. He finished it, and he urged Timothy to do the same. "Timothy, finish what you begin."

One of my favorite lines when I speak to students at Dallas Theological Seminary is this: "Don't just begin your coursework. Finish your degree. Stay with it. Don't pull away."

I say the same to you. You may be in dire straits. Times are difficult, maybe more difficult now than ever in your life. Finish the race. It's worth it all. There's a sense of satisfaction that comes when you go all the way to the end and break through the tape.

Paul fought the good fight. He finished the race. And, most importantly, he kept the faith. He stood fast for it and took blows because of it.

I've had very little persecution in my life. It's easy to think I've suffered for the gospel, until I compare myself with those who wandered about in sheepskins, who were destitute, afflicted, and tormented. They were the people of whom the world was not worthy.

I remember years ago when Swede Anderson with Campus Crusade for Christ invited me to go to the University of Oklahoma campus and speak on one of the free speech platforms. This was back during my last year at seminary. I went with him, and I stood on this free speech platform. I was doing my best to preach to people who were passing by, some standing and staring, and some sneering. All of a sudden, I got hit with a tomato!

I thought, *This is real tough persecution!*

I said, "Swede, someone threw a tomato at me!"

He said, "Yeah, isn't it exciting? It only gets better!"

You and I will know a day, quite likely, when savage times will come, and we may be incarcerated for our faith. We'll be brought before a judge, and we'll be tempted to recant. Do you know when you prepare for that moment? *Now.*

We pray with all our hearts: "Lord, give me faith. Give me the kind of internal strength that won't back down whether a rotten tomato is thrown at me or a gun is pointed in my face. Give me the courage to stand firm and not give in."

Look Forward to the Prize

If we do that, there's a marvelous future ahead. Paul wrote,

> *And now the prize awaits me—the crown of righteousness, which the Lord, the righteous Judge, will give me on the day of his return. And the prize is not just for me but for all who eagerly look forward to his appearing.* (2 Timothy 4:8)

Five crowns are named in the New Testament for five different acts of faith. This is the crown of righteousness given by the righteous Judge—unlike the human judge, Nero, who threw Paul into a dungeon. Paul trusted God to judge him rightly and give him the crown of righteousness, which we will also receive for our faith. Someday, together, as God's people in the glories of heaven, we will cast these crowns before our Lord. That time awaits us.

There's an old country song that goes like this: "Will there be any stars, any stars in my crown when at evening the sun goes down?"

Well, the answer to that is no, there won't be. There are no stars in crowns, but there are crowns. Christ will hand out rewards for a job well done. He will not overlook our efforts for Him. He will honor that in your life and in mine.

In the New Testament there are actually only two words used to distinguish two kinds of crowns (inherited versus awarded). The first is *diadema*. We get our word "diadem" from it. That's the monarch's crown—jeweled, beautiful, attractive—that often is passed from one generation to the next as the blue bloods are born into the family and take over the throne of the country. They are crowned with the *diadema*.

The other Greek work refers to a less impressive crown. It's usually of plaited leaves and ivy. Individuals would be given these crowns after an athletic event. They would stand before the *bema*, or the judgment seat, and the judge would place on their heads the *stephanos*.

Stephanos is awarded to a person due to his or her achievement. The different crowns believers receive for their different acts of faith are *stephanos* crowns. This is the type of crown Paul looked forward to receiving from his Lord.

Hand Off the Baton

You know what Paul was doing by writing 2 Timothy? He was handing off the truth like a baton to Timothy. My favorite event in the Olympics is the relay. I love it because it's a team sport. You don't run a relay alone. You run it with others, usually four in the relay, and the most critical part is the handoff of the baton.

Paul had a golden baton of truth to pass off to Timothy, and he wanted to make certain that the handoff was solid.

He told Timothy in this letter, "Hold Christ's truth high. Lift it up. Make certain you honor the Savior who has come and saved your soul. Embrace it, take it for yourself, claim it, then live it out."

His message is the same to us. Be a model of it. Don't just talk about it, live it, and pass it on. But first, guard it well, because there will be those who try to weaken the message of the truth. Stand up for it. Then, when you've prepared those who follow you to receive the truth, hand it off.

Finish Well

Paul may have been confined to a moldering dungeon, but Christ had set his spirit free. He had finished his life well, and he looked forward to the welcoming embrace of his Savior. As he lay on his rotting straw bed, he must have closed his eyes and imagined the glory that awaited him beyond the four cramped walls. With the eyes of his heart, he could envision what John described in the book of Revelation. He anticipated receiving his crown from the hand of Jesus, but then joining the heavenly hosts as they

> lay their crowns before the throne and say,
> > "You are worthy, O Lord our God,
> > to receive glory and honor and power."
> (Revelation 4:11)

We await the same experience. Someday we will join Paul as those who, "eagerly look forward to [Christ's] appearing" (2 Timothy 4:8). That will be a magnificent moment to witness, as we, who may be rewarded with a crown or two, will realize this is not about us; this is not about remembering our work. This is all about our God who gave us breath in our lungs and voices to speak and thoughts to think and a direction to go. It's all about our God.

It's all for His glory, for His purpose. That's why we were created. That's why we live. That's why we exist at this very moment. It's all part of His plan. Our life, our death, our birth, our achievements, our disappointments, our failures—whatever our days may include, it is all about the One who is worthy to receive glory and honor and praise. Nothing has a higher priority than giving glory to our God!

> *Father, we're grateful for a life that can be lived free of regret. We're grateful for the cross where we can bring our burdens, knowing that at the foot of that cross we can find forgiveness, the ability to recover, the strength to press on, the hope of eternity. Help us, our Father, in this world of woe, heartbreak, hardship, sudden surprises, and loss, to be ready as we fight the good fight. May we finish the course, not simply run it. And all the while, may we keep the faith. In the name of Jesus, we pray. Amen.*

ENDNOTES

Chapter 2—Look Within: Can You Endure Hardship?

1. Martha Snell Nicholson, "Guests," in *Poems That Preach* (Wheaton, IL: Sword of the Lord Publishers, 1952), 33.

2. Amy Carmichael, "Make Me Thy Fuel," in *Mountain Breezes: The Collected Poems of Amy Carmichael* (Fort Washington, PA: Christian Literature Crusade, 1999), 193–94. From the book *Mountain Breezes: The Collected Poems of Amy Carmichael*, copyright by The Dohnavur Fellowship and published by CLC Publications, Fort Washington, PA. Used by permission. May not be further reproduced. All rights reserved.

Chapter 5—Look Beyond: Will You Focus on Eternity?

1. Thomas Kelly, "Praise the Savior, Ye Who Know Him," Hymnary.org, hymnary.org/text/praise_the_savior_ye_who_know_him.

2. Samuel Stennett, "Majestic Sweetness Sits Enthroned," Hymnary.org, hymnary.org/text/majestic_sweetness_sits_enthroned.

3. James Russell Lowell, "The Present Crisis," in *Poems by James Russell Lowell*, vol. 2 (Cambridge: George Nichols; Boston: B. B. Mussey, and Co., 1848), 57.

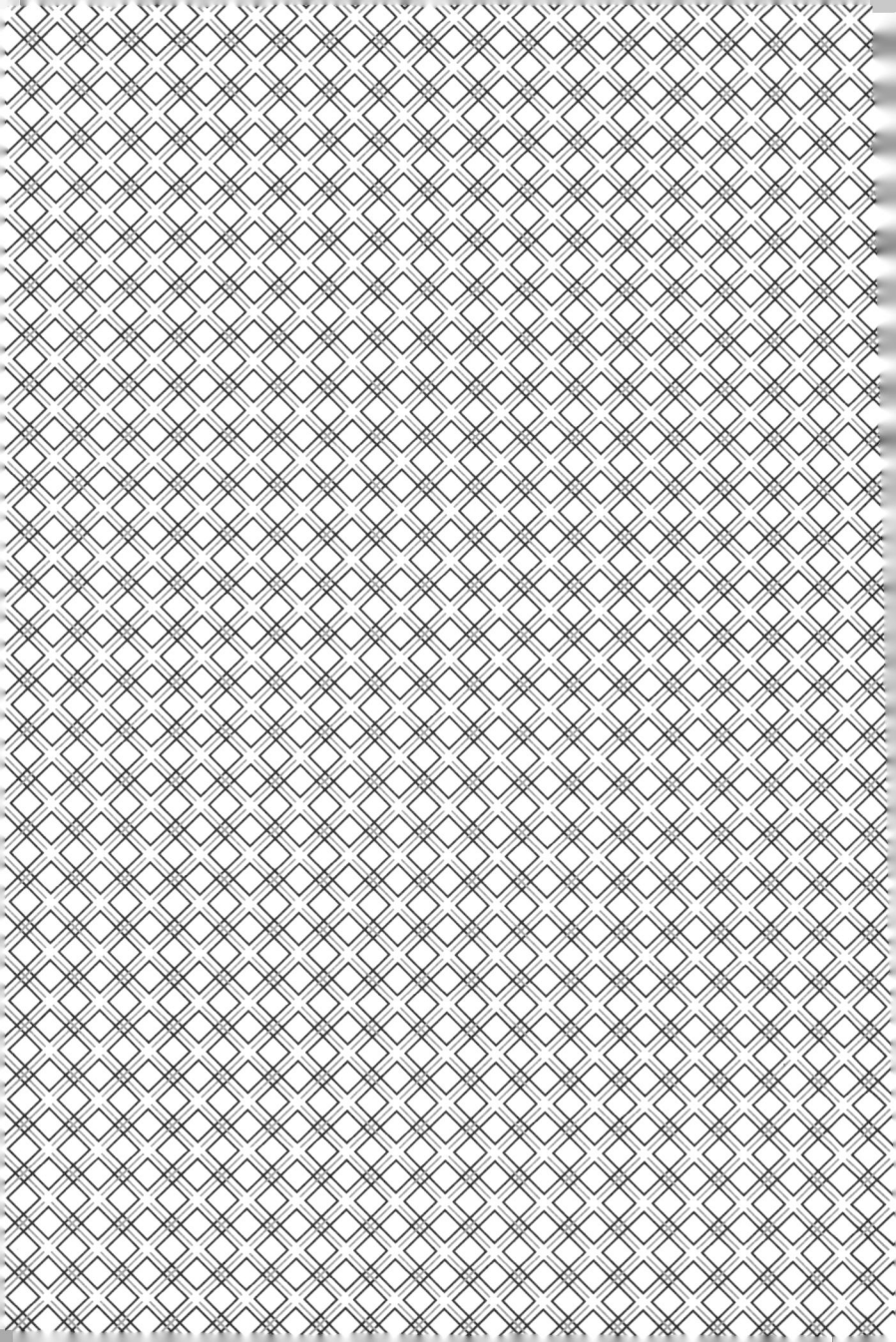